Publisher's P

Step right up! Dare to rip the gauze from your gaze! *A Newer Testament* chronicles our desperate search for the nonrepetitive and the bizarre. Can we ever get there or are we going around in circles merely? Will the mightymen maintain planet control within their bloodline? Who will eventually run their enterprises? Their jaded jetset wombfruit or their 21st Century progeny, the networking, modemized googolchips? Can uncommon sense explain away the unformulated riddles of the Sphinx? Flabbergasted by the incredibly modest success of *Misanthropology: A Florilegium of Bahumbuggery,* we have commissioned its author to respond to the swelling chorus of bahumbuggers and concoct a sequel. Attention must be paid to a neglected genre, especially when wrapped in an econoline format. This trendy bashing of Moslem fundamentalism is now accessible to those starving students slavering for the savor of neoDadaism, however sophomoric. So you see, you who have read this far, you are holding in your hands a calculated business decision. You can actually afford to buy it. Read it! Proselytize!

A Newer Testament

Misanthropology Unleashed

Reneau H. Reneau

[AUTHOR OF "MISANTHROPOLOGY: A FLORILEGIUM
OF BAHUMBUGGERY"]

Illustrations by Rogelio Naranjo

MIT DIESEM ZEICHEN
donlazaro translations
BANN' ICH DEINEN ZAUBER

Published by donlazaro translations

Printed in the United States of America by Fidlar Doubleday. No part of this book may be reproduced in any manner whatsoever without written permission except in case of brief quotations embodied in critical articles and reviews. All rights, including professional and amateur theatrical productions, motion pictures, public reading, radio and television broadcasting, and the rights of translation into foreign languages, are strictly reserved. For information, please contact: donlazaro translations, 600 E. Regent St., Inglewood, CA 90301. email: donlazaro@earthlink.net

First printing, September, 2008

Publisher's Cataloguing-in-Publication

Reneau, Reneau H.
   A Newer Testament: Misanthropology Unleashed /
   Reneau H. Reneau; illustrations by Rogelio Naranjo.

      p.cm.
      LCCN 2008906097
      ISBN   978-0-9729549-1-4

   1. Satire, American-—Miscellanea—Fiction. 2. Philosophy—Miscellanea—Fiction. 3. Cosmology—Miscellanea—Fiction.
4. Religion—Miscellanea—Fiction.
I. Naranjo, Rogelio. II. Title.

PN 6165 R46 2008   817.4

For Ariel and Tilo

By the fruits of their future ye shall know them

Contents

Foreword

A letter to the reader

Dearly Beloved;

    Five years ago Reneau H. Reneau sallied onto the literary scene with *Misanthropology: a Florilegium of Bahumbuggery,* wherein he skewered perceived wrongthinking and selfimportance. *A Newer Testament: Misanthropology Unleashed* could well be entitled *Son of a Bahumbugger,* as it provides more of the same, piled higher and deeper with more escapades involving characters introduced in the prior volume. As we are now further advanced along the timeline, we can better observe in the offing the auguries of Armageddon. Herein are explored stratagems of self-programmed machines as well as machinations of muscle-and-bone men who think like machines. This collection of "declamatory conversation" is dichotomized as "Conversations" (four garrulous fables) and "Pontifications" (two polemics).

    If HE Didn't, Who Did? takes a contemporary American Epiphany (the O.J. Trial) and massages it into the syntax of opera, exercising heartless license to twist tragic events so that they conform to the structure of Verdian libretti. It suggests concern for the direction that "spin" might take in the world of news as entertainment. Starring Yam Snosnibor and Simon Elron.

As a vehicle for smartypants Muzio Scaevola and his "loverly" Princess Laya, **So This Is Arcturus** appears to be yet another metaphor for the Voyage of Life and the distractions we contrive to make *getting there half the fun.*[i] This is a discussion of the games that people might play on a voyage that lasts literally millions of years.

In the Florilegium volume, we left Captain Snurl and Admiral Snarcesor in the Victorious Spaceship *Excelsior,* escaping from danger on the miniplanet Pluto. **Mr. Vici Forges a Coalition** picks up the adventure and soon we find the pair entangled in a web of galactic confrontation. All of earth and its family values appear to be on the verge of eclipse before a cybernetic challenge emanating from the constellation Pegasus. In cahoots is that selfmade son of a plutonian rock, Mr. Vici, who spends much of his time discussing the stuff of cosmogony with Cral Cavinu, an updated Tin Woodman of Oz.

In a salute to the colorful impact of fourletter words on American literature, #@*#!! continues the saga of Grosvenor and Bergsma, he an unlovable Dixie redneck, and she, his better Dixie half. Asar Alubat, A.A., provides gratuitous running commentary,

The Perils of Satire is a further salvo in Reneau's earnest crusade to unsully the name of L. Frank Baum, who has been accused of advocating genocide in two of his early editorials. "Not so," argues Reneau. "You don't take anything anyone says at face value without gauging the intent. The intent may reflect exactly the opposite of the literal words. Everybody flirts with sarcasm, and some actually employ reverse psychology. I've toyed with the same device myself." But be advised, folks, Reneau's intent here is straight-arrow. He presents the best case for the prosecution, and proceeds to demolish the case he honorably sets up for them.

A frightening sequence of unfortunate events is revealed in **The Bugby Legacy**. *The Institutionalized Mystic Nits*, a secret international society, describes in this document another dismal chapter from *The Protocols of the Wiseman Chazz,* its blueprint for achieving planet domination through economic terrorism. Note that here the voice of the pontificator is that of the heinous Charles Bugby.

Is there a common thread that runs through the *oeuvre* of this guru Reneau? Or does he merely potshoot at his pet peeves? Has he managed to expound a unified field of neophilosophy? None of the above, folks. Neither fake nor philosopher, he does qualify as a competent juggler of words and broker of ideas.

I have delved into and parsed both *A Newer Testament* and *Misanthropology*, emerging with three conclusions for your consideration. The first is that the devil is wise due more to his age than to his just being the devil.[ii] The second is that Reneau is so obsessed with "reverse psychology" that, although he carefully avoids it when he identifies himself as the speaker, he doesn't hesitate to employ this device through his surrogate characters. Finally, here is what I perceive to be this old devil's assessment at this stage in his game, which might go as follows: Life would be boring without variety of experience and needs to fulfill. Needs were generated at bigbang time. Some needs are usually easy to satisfy (scratch a pesky itch, or genuflect at mass to quash nagging curiosity). Some are not (put food on the table), and some are beyond our reach (use your imagination). But a mechanism exists where these too can be vicariously satisfied, even though when we leave the matinee, the sun is still out to blind us, and we are reminded that we're in Antioch, California and the war is still on. Until next Saturday, of course. And that's just the way-it-goes, as every-body-knows.[iii] We work hard to feed, clothe, and house ourselves, but manage to put aside enough for the next Saturday matinee. And herein an Old Scratch wannabe has conjured up a Saturday matinee for our diversion, leaving additional options up to us.

In the Name of the Bowels of Yahweh,

Bishop Baker

Prelate of the Bokononist persuasion
Crocker-Amazon District

---

[i] Cunard Lines slogan since days of Noah
[ii] Spanish proverb, *Mas sabe el diablo por viejo que por diablo,*
[iii] The Limeliters, *That's Just the Way It Goes*

CONVERSATIONS

If HE Didn't, Who Did?
AN OPERATIC INCURSION INTO THE BOWELS OF BAD TASTE

Nothing captured the imagination of the emotionally starved American public like the Otello (or Jago) Trial at the Turn of the Century. Moments like that provide the grist for the More Than a Century search for material that can be forged into The Great American Opera – like *Wozzeck* or *Lulu*, say, is for the Germans. *Porgy* was the pioneer that established direction, but *Susannah* sidetracked the endeavor and didn't fool anybody. Although *Klinghoffer* is back on track, its refusal to titillate us with a little illicit love precluded its steaming into the station. But wake up, opera industrialists of America: the O.J. Simpson trial has it all. Although accounts of the event already abound, Simon Elron saw Verdian metaphors pleading for an encore and felt the world was greedy for yet another version. His soon-to-be-released book is entitled *If HE Didn't, Who Did? The Doing In of Alfredo and Violetta*. It is a stylized and inventive account which in shameless abandon filches plotlines from three different Verdi masterworks with a dash of Boito for *panache*. A preview of this project follows. But don't say you weren't warned. It's a mucky arena.

CHORUS: The opening moments of Iago's soliloquy from **Otello** are heard *(Ta da da ... Credo in un Dio crudel..)*. The music fades away.

VOICE: Don't remotely entertain the notion of clicking that remote! It's roundtable time so we knight owls can josh and joust around! But here comes the Dark Prince of Knightly Arrogance himself, HARREEE CLOOTIE!

CAST: **IN ORDER OF IMPORTANCE**

CHORUS/VOICE: **BARBERSHOP TRIO**
BIGMAC MACDONALD, BASS: **IMPRESARIO**
HARRY CLOOTIE, BARITONE: INTERLOCUTOR
YAM SNOSNIBOR, MEZZO: **PUBLISHER**
SIMON ELRON, TENOR: **AUTHOR**

CHORUS: A roundtable with three empty chairs and a throne is spotlighted in centre stage, with three goblets and a chalice perched on the otherwise barren table. As a snaredrum rattles, Harry Clootie emerges from the shadowy wings. Swaggering to spotlight center, arms akimbo, he stares above the audience. The snaring suddenly stops, and the huzzahs begin. At a perceptive gesture from Clootie the din abates. Snatching the chalice, he ascends to the throne.

CLOOTIE: GREETINGS AND BLESSINGS, seekers-after-revelation, holy patrons, and NAUGHTY MUGGLES! We have assembled here tonight a VERITABLE ONSLAUGHT of preview and provocation! You all have heard rumors of the soon-to-be-released literary TELL-IT-ALL GRANDSLAM, *If HE Didn't, Who Did? The Doing In of Alfredo and Violetta*. Here with us to discuss this madding topic is the coalition team that made this combustible venture possible. Our leadoff slugger is the dauntless publisher of this MASTERPIECE OF INVESTIGATIVE REPORTING, Yam Snosnibor!

CHORUS: As each participant in this drama appears upon cue, the prompted audience performs with occasionally inappropriate noise.

CLOOTIE: Now stepping up to the plate is her boss, that daunting mogul of the Fourth Estate, MOVER-AND-SHAKER Macdonald, Chairman and CEO of the universally feared BigMac Media!

CHORUS: As the catcalls subside, Big Mac flashes a defiant sign-of-the-street to the crowd and seats himself. The snaredrum again does its thing, stopping suddenly as Clootie raises an eyebrow.

CLOOTIE: And here's the 2004 CALDECOTT AWARDWINNER for *Bionosis: the Art of Auto-Delusion*, listed in Guinness as the GREATEST

BOOK OF THE WESTERN WORLD! Now proudfather of a new preordained classic, let's RING THE NOBEL for the Babe Ruth of our lineup, the wittingly CONTROVERSIAL **SIMON ELRON**!

CHORUS: Pandemonium. Security guards have to intervene to quash the euphoria reigning in the otherwise ruly bleachers. Clootie quickly bottomups the chalice. Elron waves, bows, salutes, points to center field, and sits down. There is an abrupt silence of anticipation.

CLOOTIE: Sorry, Simon, that your wife Simone couldn't be with us today to SHARE YOUR TRIUMPH. But a little Diddly-Dickie bird told me she's very busy these days performing undercover terrorist activities for the CIA. A family of multitalent! By now, everyone in the world knows that your book is due to HIT THE STANDS next week. NO ONE ANYWHERE, especially among the chatty Sunnis in the gossip markets of Tikrit, TALKS OF ANYTHING ELSE. Another fourbagger for the SULTAN OF SWAT! Tonight we will reveal the secrets in this GREATEST YARN SINCE THE BOOKS OF MOSES! Simon Elron will tell us his titillating conclusion, before the book is even released to the street! REMEMBER, YOU HEARD IT HERE! Tell us, Simon, did you perform extensive and excruciating research before coming to your SNAP JUDGEMENT?

SIMON: First let me say hi! to my mom and to all you autodeluded fans out there. I wouldn't be Number

One in Guinness without your victory votes cast at the Amazon.com till. But you nailed it, Harry. Extensive research can get excruciating. Better to go with that still silent voice within and get the job done. Decide on a conclusion, stick with it, and you'll find that the facts you were going to garner are already rounding third.

CLOOTIE: CANNY INTUITION, I call it. However, even before your SOLIDLY DOCUMENTED conclusion has been made known, AS IT WILL INDEED BE REVEALED LATER ON THIS VERY SHOW, we have heard mutterings from squirmers out there, no doubt with GUILTY CONSCIENCES. Rumbles of *libel* and *lawsuit* are in the air! Are you prepared to confront your accusers in court?

SIMON: At worst, it'll be a Pyrrhic defeat for me, Harry. More embarrassing notoriety for the plaintiff, more sales for the defendant. I say, BRING 'EM ON! -- to the public pillory.

CLOOTIE: What do you say to that, Yam Snosnibor? You're the publisher. Even if IRRESPONSIBLE deprecations thrust this book IN THE FACES of eager buyers, can you afford to ignore looming lawsuits and boycotts? One angry mustachioed man was even heard to mutter, *"Sii maledetto!"*

YAM: Actually, my boss, Big Mac, is the target for the curses and court actions. He's the greenbackadolla guy, and his hide is pretty impervious to any *maledizione*. I come to you with the purest of motives. It's not the money, sonny. I simply believe in free speech, and welcome every opportunity to defend and promote it. Folks have a Constitutional Right to be exposed to outrageous and exciting ideas. Simon Elron has a story to tell. I'm proud to be an enabler when it comes to freedom of expression.

BIG MAC: A hypocrite I'm not, Clootie. Of course I expect to come out of this with a fatbottom line. As for Mr. Mustachio, a big fat scoff for his *maledizione*. Yes; Snosnibor, Elron and I come to the table with different perspectives, but we all see a positive benefit to the nation in the publication of this long overdue opus. It will be a breath of air freshener! My PR lackeys assure me that we have nothing to fear from frivolous lawsuits; our task is to entice negotiables from the wallets of the illiterati, and convince these yokels that they will want to be able to comment knowingly on this Pillar of Western Literature at their water cooler or sewing circle. We are making it easier for any conscientious objectors out there by announcing that a portion of the proceeds, no matter how small, will go to charity. Community involvement is a calculated tradition at BigMac Media.

SIMON: The climate is ripe for a revisionist look at the Trial of the Twentieth Century. Folks are ready to challenge the judgments of their forefathers and examine shocking new verdicts. I am but the amanuensis for their hidden musings.

CLOOTIE: And here tonight, you latenite telepeepers will be the FIRST ON THE BLOCK to break the news to your office cohorts! WHO DONE IT??? Just hang in there. In the meantime, many of us are excited about some of Miss Snosnibor's other civic enterprises, and we would be DERELICT not to TAKE ADVANTAGE of her presence here tonight and confront her with our RIGHT-TO-KNOWITALL! I understand you are the founder of a national freedom of speech club, a kind of NRA for First Amendment junkies. SPEAK FREELY!

YAM: You refer to The Voltaire Society, the *FIRE* in the Belle of Liberty. We are the perennial patriots; we're at the ramparts, come avalanche or drought, fighting to the death for anyone's right to say whatever.

CLOOTIE: My prompter tells me Voltaire didn't say that.

YAM: Did I say he did? No matter. It embodies his spirit, and as such is a challenge and an inspiration for all of us.

BIG MAC: But you can't mean that literally, my dear. Of course, if you weren't an exuberant idealist I wouldn't have hired you in the first place. It signals spark and spunk. However, if you're still spouting sedition after working for me awhile, I can fire you anytime.

CLOOTIE: OUCH! Incidentally, my prompter tells me you're a plagiarist.

BIG MAC: Did I say I wasn't? Fire your prompter. If you don't, I'll buy your network and fire him myself. As for you, my dear Snosnibor, while our little magnum opus clearly falls under the aegis of free speech, does free speech protect a man falsely shouting "fire!" in a crowded theatre? No freedom is absolute. This was established back in 1919 to quench the flames of anarchy.

YAM: Mr. Mac, you're so lost in space. Why bother with "falsely?" If the point is that people would be trampled, the result would be the same, fire or no fire. Wouldn't it be preferable to educate folks to calmly file out of the designated exits in the event of any perceived danger? Folks can be educated to obediently send their sons and daughters to shoot and be shot in dubious battles. Can't they be educated to march out of a theater like good soldiers, even when under fire? A little education is a powerful tool. Your old "fire!" saw was cranked out by a sitdown clown who landed a lifetime gig on the Supreme Court and suddenly found his oneliners becoming the law of the land.

SIMON: Yo! Thanks to this flip jurisprude the cause for free speech has been afflicted with an impediment ever since. Vigilantes have used that metaphor to justify a sustained attack on the First Amendment, proclaiming that a wolf is at the door, or may be at the door, or that somewhere a wolf is thinking about it. Or might think about it in the very near future. We of the Voltaire Society dare not accept any limit at all on free speech.

CLOOTIE: Then EXTREMISM IN THE DEFENSE OF LIBERTY IS NO VICE? That's what Barry-the-Revolutionary said. Was he RIGHT ON TARGET OR WHATNOT?

SIMON: Tyranny in the defense of democracy is oxymoronic. Don't bait me. We simply mean that Congress shall make no law abridging the freedom of speech. Admittedly a revolutionary idea.

YAM: The NRA takes the same position regarding Amendment Number Two. It's no coincidence that it immediately follows Amendment Number One. Only these fatcat guys take no prisoners. And you can't say they haven't accomplished their goals, in spite of the casualties occasioned by firearms proliferation. Anyway, we can agree with them about eternal vigilance.   All civil liberties are derivative of the right to say and read whatever you want to. Take *that* property away and there's nothing left of any value in the portfolios of the skinnycats.

BIG MAC: The Right-to-Riflers have deeper pockets than do you Free-Speechies. That might explain the sweet smell of their success. But don't come preaching around my door with your collection plate. The Voltaire Society is your baby, not mine. I say let's get on with the business at hand. You know I don't have time to read anything, much less all the swill I dump into the publicmedia trough. Tell us who really, REALLY did it, Yam. You've even got *me* curious.

CLOOTIE: HOLD YOUR HORSES, everybody! We're getting there! I think that it corresponds to Simon Elron, who did all the GRUNTWORK for *If HE Didn't, Who Did? The Doing In of Alfredo and Violetta* to reveal to us his GRANDSLAM conclusion, and how he got there. Of course we understand that for the juicy details we'll need to buy a copy next Tuesday, available in every newsstand and supermarket on the planet. THE WORLD IS WAITING, Simon Elron; WHAT'S YOUR CALL?

SIMON: I knew when I tackled this project that I was invading an already pillaged territory, where conventional wisdom warns, "Be sure to invest in a roundtrip ticket all ye who take this trip. There's precious little more that people want to hear about the Otello/Jago trial."

YAM: Little do those wiseacres know. They're the same wags that insist that property is not theft. I respond in the raging baritone of Cochran the crackerjack, "Truth forever on the scaffold, falsehood ever on the throne!"

SIMON: The responsibility for the murders of Alfredo and Violetta lies squarely at the feet of a tragic figure. His name is Giorgio Germont, and he's Alfredo's dad. I'll tell you how and why.

CHORUS: From the bleachers, clogged with homosaps, there went up the noisy mumble of disorganized protest. As near as we could tell, it was an olio of "No way!" and "What th'?" and "How's that??" with an occasional "Wha'd I tell y', maw?"

CLOOTIE: Due to the TRANSCENDENTAL NATURE of these revelations our sponsors have waived the time for their commercials until the end of the show.

Please EXPLAIN YOURSELF, Simon Elron. This is shocking BEYOND HUMAN KEN.

SIMON: I'll give you the barebones chronology. Of course you'll want the bareflesh details, and my mudrasslin' research has bared it all! The unexpurgated edition goes on sale next Tuesday at an outlet near you. Get a copy before it's yanked off the shelves! This is my solidly documented account: Giorgio Germont learned that his son Alfredo was seeing Violetta Valéry d'Otello, rumored to be a reincarnation of Ezekiel's ho Aholibah. Germont was understandably concerned that this relationship would not only sully the future of his son, but also undermine his own influence in the community. One day while in the dentist's office he was perusing an issue of ***Mossad Soldier of Fortune*** and an ad caught his eye: "PEST EXTERMINATION SERVICES. KOSHER AND DISCREET. CALL HYMIE SPARAFUCILE & ASSOCIATES." An inquiry soon led to an arrangement with a hitman of integrity, whose credentials indicated that he had always fulfilled his obligations in full compliance with the ethics of his profession. He was contracted by Giorgio Germont to take care of Violetta Valéry d'Otello.

CLOOTIE: I DON'T NEED TO TELL YOU, Simon Elron, that you'd best be able to BACK UP THESE INCENDIARY ALLEGATIONS with more than your still, silent voice.

SIMON: I interviewed a gentleman who, while burglarizing the Germont residence two days prior to the incident, overheard a discussion of the entire plot in an adjoining room. The following remark assaulted his ear, from a voice sounding to him like that of a middleaged, mustachioed male Semite: "Slit the N-word f**king/lovin *itch." My witness stated that at that moment a dog started wailing accusingly, and he had to leave.

CLOOTIE: And just where is this gentleman informant today?

SIMON: He had business to attend to in El Salvador. But I took the precaution to videotape the interview.

CLOOTIE: WOULDN'T YOU KNOW IT. I trust you have other bolstering facts, untainted by HEARSAY. These are WILDY INFLAMMATORY ALLEGATIONS, involving SPECIAL CIRCUMSTANCES! Ethnic enclaves are collectively finetuned to detect DISRESPECT, however gross.

YAM: Yes, yes! Race provides just one of various opportunities for solidarity, for mass pride and mass indignation, for mutual support and congratulation, a convenient escape from individual responsibility. Identification with a group manifests itself in different avenues, conventionally in allegiance to a football team, to a country, to a religion. Pride in your football team? In your ethnicity? What do you have to do with the accomplishments of poets and philosophers who happen to look like you? They will always differ from you in one overriding respect: they've accomplished something. Group allegiance does work as a powerful instrument for those who would manipulate the masses. Race is one of the divide-and-rule trump cards in the wealth-and-power game.

SIMON: Well, even if an individual accomplishes nothing tangible by himself, isn't it possible that the artist is an eloquent vehicle for group expression, and without the group would have nothing to express?

YAM: Maybe so. But I say, so what. When nudge comes to push, what matters most: country, education, religion, or money in the bank? Why did "women and children first" only apply to firstclass women and firstclass children on the Titanic, regardless of race, ethnicity, or country of origin? The firstclass Prussian and the firstclass Brit waltzed away to the lifeboats while behind locked iron gates the thirdclass Kraut and the thirdclass Limey, with their thirdclass babes in tow, haplessly hokeypokied to the bottom of the sea. And that's what it's all about.

BIGMAC: Bolshevik!

YAM: Well, what alternative is there? Sadducee aristocrats point to the ants and the bees and say, "Look, that's just the way it is. Now lick my boots and may God bless." Enlightened Pharisees point to the ants and the bees and say, "Look, we all prosper from a share-the-wealth society. Now lick my boots and I'll give you a shiny quarter."

SIMON: And as to the Estate of the Lords Spiritual, orthodox crackpottery indeed leaches into the picture. I discovered that Giorgio Germont was enrolled in a radical sect that has allowed some credence to be attached to a pornographic horror entitled ***The***

Chronicles of Yahweh, starring a bearded old ogre of that name, AKA Yaweh. I procured a copy of this document and read a chilling episode where some fundamentalist fanatic was on the verge of murdering his own son because Yahweh had ordered him to do so. He was stopped from consummating this cockamamie deed when an angel of Yahweh suddenly appeared in the nickotime and assured this obedient idiot, who was just following orders, that he was just kidding. In this same chronicle, ladies of pleasure and their patrons are persistently hounded and destroyed by Yahweh and his agents in what can only be described as an unholy holocaust. In one horrible orgy of wholesale ethnic cleansing, every man, woman, and child on the planet, with the exception of one suckup *übermenschen* family, is drowned because of some perceived mass iniquity. Yahweh really makes Dubya and DiddlyDick look like gnatweights.

CLOOTIE: Did your informant CONVENIENTLY take this ghastly chronicle with him on his flight to El Salvador?

SIMON: I have that same testament in my very hand at this very moment! You'll find it a veritable florilegium of cant and rant that pushes the envelope of free speech. Even the Marquis de Sade failed in his attempts to come up with something more outrageous. Now, would you trust someone who worships at the altar of this monster Yahweh? It would be impudent and presumptuous for anyone to proclaim a morality superior to that of the gods that he serves. This pornosaga is our Exhibit "A." The

SimiValley Centurions who protect and serve in L.A. took the easy way out, framing "jealous" exhubby Otello for the murder of Violetta and her latest flame, Alfredo. But what really nails the lid on the coffin of all the planted evidence in this case is my debunking of the linchpin of the prosecution's fabrications: the anonymous remark overheard in a men's room at LAX by an expert witness, "The Juice did it." The D.A.'s office was able to convince everyone but the jury that this referred to the defendant Otello. It took alot of mindbending for them to come up with a reasonable beyond doubt explanation of the "J," you may recall. They laboriously demonstrated that the "J" referred to "Jago," which was the name that Otello's orchestrator Giuseppe had planned for his opus prior to the actual baptism; ergo, O(J), or "The Juice." What a crock! The remark, in fact, was simply that "*the Jews did it*." I mean like the rest is just commonsense, as disjointed circumstance morphs into eloquent evidence.

CLOOTIE: *DIO!* You are saying that this Sparafucile fellow WASTED Violetta, but before he could leave, Alfredo came up the walk, and Sparafucile was obliged to DISPATCH the innocent Alfredo as well?

SIMON: Not quite. The truth is juicier. Briefly, this is what happened: Alfredo gets Violetta pregnant, just as his passion for her begins to cool. Earlier, it is rumored, he had surprised Violetta serving up the Brentwood Hello to her illegalalien gardener. Furthermore, he knows his dad will be furious if his own liaison with this shady lady continues. Unaware of his father's arrangement, Alfredo decides to eliminate her and to his eternal honor at least does not contract out his own dirtywork. Unfortunately for Alfredo, Sparafucile appears at the inopportune moment, and feeling honorbound to fulfill his covenant one way or another (ignorant of the relationship of Alfredo to his client), in turn he tranquilizes Alfredo.

CLOOTIE: CUT! HOLD IT, Simon. You're SPINNING OUT OF CONTROL with outrageous hypothesis, my lad, and procreating calumny. As I recall, Alfredo had announced to a tableful of witnesses that he was on his way to visit Violetta that very evening. It DEFIES ALL COMMONSENSE to inform everybody that you're on the way to the scene of the crime that you're about to commit.

SIMON: Precisely, my dear Clootie! You've just countered your own objection. This Alfredo was a diabolical practitioner of reverse psychology. You want evidence? All documented in my book, but there are three conclusive eyewitness accounts that remove all reasonable doubt from the case against young Germont.   (1) Although the Coroner's Office dutifully suppressed information concerning her pregnancy, Violetta appeared to be "pretty chubby" (ha, ha) to a waitress at Norm's in Santa Monica just a week prior to her demise. I have the deposition of that waitress. When sales of my book begin to ebb, she will publish her salacious dissertation for a PhD in Political Science at Pepperdine based on her canny observations, *Iago Was Right After All: How Cassio Diddled Shakespeare*. (2) Apparently Alfredo had become romantically entangled with a fading but very wealthy Hollywood actress. A drinkinbuddy of Alfredo's avers that a pinup of Liz Taylor suddenly appeared in Alfredo's bathroom at about the same time that he was losing interest in Violetta. (3) Alfredo had written a book report on **An American Tragedy** for his English 100 class, and that same drinkinbuddy seems to recall him commenting, "That sissy Monty Clift's mistake was his M.O.; he should have used a razor in a dark alley." You've got the grisly picture. I rest my case.

CLOOTIE: WOWIE! You've got AN ANSWER FOR EVERYTHING! I guess as DEVIL'S ADVOCATE I've yet to sprout my horns. And that scalawag Hymie Sparafucile, UNDER WHAT ROCK is *he* hiding?

SIMON: He's out there somewhere in the jungleland of the Semite mafia. Otello has sworn to devote his life to turning over every rock in creation until he uncovers the rascal, after he finally settles accounts with Germont in a court of law.

BIG MAC: The whole thing stinks of Semite bashing to me. Some of my best lawyers have funny hats and jawbeavers, or uncles that do. You're making sport of these earnest gentlemen. Unfortunately for you, I now own everything in sight, and you neoNazis are all fired.

CLOOTIE: It's a TRIPLE PLAY! You're out!! You're out!! What th'?? *I'm* out!!

S, Y & C: *Sii maledetto,* you old fart!

CHORUS: As the curtain slowly closes, Simon, Yam, and Clootie point accusingly at BigMac. The snaredrum begins a sinister rattle. BigMac's gaze turns defiantly upward. When the curtain closes, a period from the big bassdrum stops the chatter of the snare. A guffaw from BigMac is heard from behind the curtain, and now brandishing a bright red trident he steps out to heckle the audience.

BIG MAC: *La maledizione?* I'm in charge of that department, too. You uppity moonbeamers who snipe at our institutions will come crawling back with more respect for us hardnosed oligarchs. We are the ones who guide your lives and provide for your sustenance, in return for a bit of your blood, toil, tears and sweat. In the meantime, you can beef up the humility quotient in your *curricula* by attending the reality seminars offered in soup kitchens and unemployment lines. Freedom? Slavery? Just a state of mind. *Fischio! Fischio! Fischio!*

CHORUS: As the Mephistophelean BigMac moves back and forth, he whistles and hisses violently. The orchestra picks up the Iago soliloquy approaching its final bars, and continues to *"E veccia fola il Ciel ... ha ha ha."* The lights are dimmed, and suddenly extinguished.

So This Is Arcturus!

What does it take to accomplish great deeds? Can watching the Dr. Deceit show or highlighting every other paragraph of *Awakening the Genius Within* lead you up the path to stardom? Do you really think so? Can you live the good life by paying attention to nongeniuses who have achieved their good life by taking our money to tell us how to live a good life, but otherwise would be in the same boat as we are? Can you really swallow their elixirs? We all know deep down that geniuses are not made, but born. We would like to think otherwise, which is why we are so drawn to fantasies evoking imagery of sow's-ears-to-silk-purse morphogenesis. Geniuses are often annoying, because they are obviously superior to you and me, and they know it. The very idea disses politicalcorrectness and rankles our fragile selfesteem. But these are the ones who will engineer our future. The rest of us carry hods of bricks. This is the story of one of those annoying engineers. As you will see, he accomplishes marvelous things. But, as you will also note, he accepts that it's no fun to go it alone. So maybe as catalysts we may indeed be an indispensable element in the genius process.

SO THIS IS ARCTURUS !

ACT I: The curtain does not move, but dancing points of light are projected on it as the opening bars from *Ride of the Valkyries* are heard. The curtain then rises on the empty control room of the spaceship *Exodus*, now less than ten minutes but more than ten thousand miles from the earth. Wagner softly retreats, and through a paneless window between the control room and the adjoining game room Muzio Scaevola and Princess Laya are seen transfixed on an unseen Eidoideator, from which the voice of the Princess is apparently emanating:

(VOICE OF LAYA): *"Lo, the darting bowling orb! Lo, the brother orbs around, all the clustering suns and planets, all the dazzling days, all the mystic nights with dreams, Pioneers! O pioneers!"*

```
CAST OF CHARACTERS:

CHORUS:            ENTERTAINERS IN THEIR OWN RIGHT,
                   CHARGED WITH KEEPING YOU AWAKE
MUZIO SCAEVOLA:    ADMIRAL OF THE OPEN SKY
PRINCESS LAYA:     HIS CHEERY SPACE COMPANION
ASAR ALUBAT:       EGO ENHANCER
REDDY MILLIWIT:    TECHIE
COMPUTER PROGRAM:  FILIUS EX MACHINA
```

CHORUS: Dr. Muzio Scaevola, A.K.A. "Lefty" Scaevola, is in the spaceworthy craft

Exodus, together with his spacemate, the lovely Princess Laya, on their merry spaceway to Arcturus. Scaevola turns off the Eidoideator with his wizard wand, and he and Laya enter the control room to mime the action we describe as we speak. He and a staybehind cadre of selfless *Mystic Nits,* an organization founded by Scaevola to establish efficient autocratic government and monitor proper conduct of the citizenry, had labored for months on the *Exodus*, a marvel of galactic age engineering. It was built in a secret subterranean hideaway somewhere in Rhode Island, where it never occurred to anyone in the F. B. of I. to look for it. Scaevola, normally a giant leap ahead of the rest of mankind and feeling totally bogged down by stubborn and inferior minds, has decided to strike out for himself to populate another corner of the universe with a race of pretty smarties and genius hunkies. In spite of his having successfully accomplished the scientific scoop of the decade, the development of the incredibly versatile Philosopher's Stone *(ta-da!)* -- that can convert protons, electrons, neutrons, etcetera from any substance to *any other substance!* -- he has been given the dirty digit. The Stone *(ta-da!)* accomplishes transformation without beep or atomic explosion, thus maximizing the mass of desired output product and reducing to zero any radioactive fallout. Certainly calling for a Nobel Prize or at least an honorary degree. Anything but the patronizing Slap-on-the-Back that they emailed him. But what he had accomplished was not what the World Bank had in mind, and he found himself a prophet without honor on his own planet. And when he appealed to the Court of Public Opinion by clogging up the Internet with his Manifesto, they put out a contract on him. *Just so long can genius,* as an equally unappreciated bard once complained, *please the talentgang.* Scaevola, hoodwinking the feds with a robot lookalike, has taken off for other climes with his chatroom playmate, Princes Laya. He has stashed away in the ship's larder some gold ingots for transformation into victuals, which should last for several years. When the ingots are all consumed, he intends to forage along the spacetrail, casting out an ethernet to capture wandering space rubble and asteroid chips for transformation into square meals and lollipops as needed. Anyway, right now they're just 10 minutes into what promises to be a long flight -- and another first for the Guinness. Laya and Scaevola enter the control room.

LAYA: Omigod! Y'r Eye-doh-idi-whatever is like totally cool, Muzzie! It took th' notion right outa me yapper an' spun it inta such el'gant yadda yadda!

SCAEVOLA: Just one of many amazing amenities of my own invention that await you on this voyage, my tiddly winkie. Glad to be of service and gladder that it's appreciated. Instead of just parrying Valleyjabber between gulps, we can celebrate quality conversations worthy of André Gregory! Just point the wizard wand to the Eidoideator, click the "Spin" button, conjure up a thought, and it'll translate the thought, however pedestrian, into soaring poetry, and in your own voice. And there's more! Every evening after supper we'll foreplay over a fifth of *Hornitos* and watch an episode or two of *I Love Lucy* while we revel.

LAYA: I can't believe what's bouncin' roun' me earlobes! Y' brought along all ten thousan' showtimes o' *I Love Lucy* in y'r fannypack?

SCAEVOLA: All the repertory of Desilu ten thousandfold wouldn't crack the span of eons we'll spend together in heterorapture, my bonnie bunny. I brought along two episodes: the one with Harpomarx and of course her Guzzlers' Gin spinoff. Why waste precious spaceship space on lesser stuff?

LAYA: Are y' out o' gray matter, Muzzie me rutty rabbit? Even "Th' Star Spangle Banner" gets tiresome after two hearin's.

SCAEVOLA: Not to worry! Built into each episode is a subliminal suggestion that makes us forget the entire episode. It's a revelation to us on the morrow, and we'll watch them anew daily.

LAYA: I couldn'a hitched meself to a man more ahead o' th' herd! Hip hip hooray fer me Muzzie.

SCAEVOLA: And when we do finally get to Arcturus, we'll rejuvenate that decrepit old cosmic joke and exercise dominion over it and all its environs with vigor and confidence. A new race of men shall come forth in the stars, with the vision of Nestor and the beauty of Helen!

LAYA: But what if it works out th' other way, Muzzie? Like, I'm no G.B.S., but you totally ain't no Isadora, lovie. Y'know what I'm sayin'?

SCAEVOLA: Always belittling! Alas, after exchanging our eternal vows, you've morphed from the succulent Helen into the peevish Xanthippe! And I from the noble Nestor to the *buffo* Don Pasquale. I shall ideate in due haste a sweet personality pill that will transform you into a loving and dutiful wife, as befitting your role as the mother of *la civilización de la vanguardia.*

LAYA: F'real? Just hold it right there an' gimme a break. Do y' wanna roboLaya or a hot human wife? I am what I am. Take me as is or leave me as is. An' y' don't dazzle me one bitty glimmer with y'r airs o' Mexicano cavalero.

SCAEVOLA: I, Dr. Scaevola, scourge of simpletons, who once
            held all Foggybottom atremble, am but lackey to
            your whims! But be nice to me. We've a long trek
            ahead. Let us celebrate our successful launch
            together and consummate a bit of marital bliss this
            same enchanted eventide!

LAYA: Not so fas', swee' prince. Me mum told me t' just
            wait 'til we get t' Arcturus. As comfy as it is, this
            spacecraf' is no place for a nurs'ry. Y' won't have
            the time to daddy around and still kayo all th'
            evildoers aboundin' out there. Y' know what I'm
            sayin'? Besides, half th' titillation is gettin' there.

SCAEVOLA: You don't know what YOU are saying, my feisty
            filly. It will take us a really, really long time to get
            to Arcturus, even with the blackhole accelerator I
            devised. But not to worry, we can stave off any
            nursery complications and still not be mired in
            anticipation.

LAYA: Dr. Scaevola, am I readin' y' right? Did y' leave
            your hifalutin idealism back in Rhode Island? Did y'
            know that 'way back in th' Firs' Book o' Moses, God
            Hisself wasted a man called Onan f'r blasphemin'
            like that? Y'r materialist power t' manip'late atoms
            may be worth a zillion buckos, but y'r immortal soul
            -- like, priceless. Y'know what I'm sayin'? And like
            if hellfire don't mean nothin' to y', at least respec' th'
            faith o' me sainted mum.

SCAEVOLA: Can this be the same "Blue Angel" I courted in the
            playmate.com chatroom? The Princess who
            dreamed of blasting off into space with a Man for
            All Seasons? The Princess who was the star

entertainer at Pinocchio's of Pleasure Island? Could it be that you saw me as a quick trip to the world of diamonds and gold that you knew I could create for you with a snippetysnap? I weep in disillusion.

LAYA: Whatever. I brought along a Giant Search-A-Word book that should keep me occupied f'r an eon. Y' should be like totally ecstatic that I'm inta educatin' me head. In the whileaway, you'd better figure out some other way t' amuse y'rself, unless y' wanna spend th' whole trip in one of those cryofridge boxes in th' Absolutely Cold Pantry. Me mum gave me a Five Bonnie Yarmulkes game t' bring along and find out if y' really know how many beans make five. She picked it up at th' last meetin' of her Mensa support group. It takes four people t' play at it, so it'll have to wait 'til we get t' Arcturus, I calc'late. Like, didn't y' bring anythin' besides me t' pass the time?

SCAEVOLA: Oh misery! My *suegra mensa* haunts me in outer space. My Blue Angel Laya, I can simply invent amusements as we speed along our route. And surely my Eidoideator is good for many stimulating stellar evenings. You yourself appeared to be cavorting with Walt Whitman on his *Leaves of Grass* for a moment there. And you haven't seen yet what the Eidoideator can do to jolt the dimensions of your perception. Trust me! Confronted with mockery, my distress is yet mollified by infatuation, so I propose an armistice until I can devise an argument you can't refute. How about a round of charades? Any number can play. With my ingenuity, those cryofridges will never have any appeal.

LAYA: F'real? Sounds like a phat move, Cap'n Daddy-O! Y' see, we *can* get along just like merry ol' space mariners until we get t' Arcturus. An' then the stars will like blush at th' r'splendence of our passion! Trus' me.

SCAEVOLA: *Sale y vale, mi vida.* That's Latinlover palaver for *you're on, my pet.* Ladies first.

LAYA: Subjec', movie titles.

CHORUS: Laya holds up her index finger.

SCAEVOLA: One word.

CHORUS: Laya nods and holds up index and middle fingers.

SCAEVOLA: Two syllables.

CHORUS: Laya nods, again holds up the index finger, and starts moving around in a quick march but with baby steps, ulnae parallel to the ground, hands in fist formation, and moving in tandem with her feet. Every few steps she stops, puckers her lips open, moves the right fist up and down, and then continues her choppy dancestep.

SCAEVOLA: Got it! Train!

CHORUS: Laya nods in a nay way, but motions encouragingly that he's on the right track. She continues her marchy dancestep, but stops more frequently, looking at Scaevola significantly as she move her right forearm up and down and puckers her lips.

SCAEVOLA: Choo?

CHORUS: Laya raises her hands in dismay, shakes her head nay, nay, nay, and tries another tack. She stands straight, holds her left fist in front of her mouth, and her right fist in front of the first. Then she again puckers her lips, opens her right fist, and moves the fingers one after another, downup, downup, downup, downup. Scaevola laughs, claps his hands happily and says

SCAEVOLA: Got it! It's TOOT!

CHORUS: Laya nods yea! and smiles. She holds up two fingers, then a single finger, and continues. This time she puts her open palm just above her eyes, like a lowflying salute, and suddenly points with her left hand to something out yonder.

SCAEVOLA: Yes! Yes! It's SEE! The movie is TOOTSIE! But your first clue was a bummer.

LAYA: I can't believe it tookya so long, Mr. quotequote Genius quotequote. Like I can beatcha I betcha.

CHORUS: Scaevola holds up three fingers, then two, and two again.

LAYA: Three words, secon' word, two syllables.

CHORUS: Scaevola purses his lips downward, scrunches his eyes, makes a V with index and middle digits of his left hand, and moves up and down pointing at eyes and cheeks.

LAYA: It's CRYIN', y' fool. Needn' waste any more of your genius time. TH' CRYIN' GAME! Now gimme me gol' medal.

SCAEVOLA: Avast, my churly chickadee, you must understand that the winner in charades is the one who, as the mime, can limn with clarity the wordless message! I'm afraid, my dearest loser, that the gold goes to your unchivalrous husband, sworn to uphold righteousness, however devastating to your selfesteem. But I don't mind sharing the credit. An asterisk is yours in the ship's log!

LAYA: I can't believe me hearholes! Th' great Scaevola, a cheatin', chauvinist pig! Jus' kiddin', Muzzie. But this game don't work f'r jus' two play'rs. If y' win, y' lose, if y' lose y' win. Like, tha's no fun.

CHORUS: A guffaw is heard, stifled, but nonetheless a guffaw, and clearly not from Princess Laya or Dr. Scaevola, or you wouldn't be hearing about it from us.

SCAEVOLA: I beg your pardon?

LAYA: It's not mine f'r th' beggin'. Like, they's chiggers in th' furniture! I spy a wiggle 'neath th' *étagère*!

CHORUS: Reddy Milliwit and Asar Alubat emerge from behind the *étagère*. They are notorious U.S. Government secret agents. While back on bugbog, they had failed in their assignment to bring Scaevola to justice for his subversive activity, pouncing instead on a robot lookalike of Scaevola's manufacture, thus allowing the real Scaevola to escape to outer space. A contract was issued by the FB of I for the heads of Milliwit and Alubat.

SCAEVOLA: Why, it's Mr. Megapoop and Señor Alubat! What are you two finks doing here? What's happeneeeng, Bato? *Explícate.*

ALUBAT: We can explain, O great Chairman of the Select People's Quorum Reglamentarians! Just give us a nonce to get our story straight.

MILLIWIT: Yea, we come bearing explanations.

SCAEVOLA: You are messing up my expedition, you charlinoodles! This craft was not constructed for a foursome! To correct in flight is a challenge even for me.

MILLIWIT: We are fleeing for our lives. When we botched the job trying to turn you in for due process, their wrath turned upon us, and we were doomed to plugged nickeldom.

SCAEVOLA: But how did you find my R.I. hideaway?

MILLIWIT: Aha! Ask Princess "Blue Angel." She was MY eplaybunny until you came along. She spilled the beans in the Dear John she enailed to my edoor.

LAYA: What th'! *You're* "Cap'n Underpants?"

MILLIWIT: Bygones are auld lang syne. We're all in the same spaceboat now. And hey, we surrender, o Great Mystic Nit. We just want to join your crew. We can all be friends. Yesterday's nuts are today's mighty oaks like you, boss.

SCAEVOLA: Ye are the scum of the earth, ye unclean scum! Hark, if your earwax will permit it. I shall open the escape hatch and you shall skedaddle! Get lost in the ether.

ALUBAT: Consider! Your conscience will bug you all the way to Arcturus. Guilt will hamper your most intimate daily functions! Besides, wouldn't we be useful in the event of any need for clinical trials? We could nibble local vegetation to check for deadly venom. Or you could inoculate us first with any unproven serum that you may ideate for some unforeseen calamity. Priceless! That's what we are.

SCAEVOLA: You just don't capeesh the scope of my genius, do you? But you may be right about the conscience bit. I do have a heart at least as big as my head. Stay, then, repent and make yourselves useful. There are pots to be washed in the scullery. Begone.

MILLIWIT: We can make the long, tedious journey a rollicking one! We have brought along a couple of decks of cards and can while away the eons playing bridge! The pots can wait, let's choose our partners and get started! I pick the Princess.

LAYA: What kind o' floozy do y' take me f'r, Cap'n Smelly? Bicker we may, but Muzzie's me hubby, and if there's any partnerin', he's mine. Y'know what I'm sayin'? An' if th' pots can wait, so can th' bridge. Now we can play me mum's Five Bonnie Yarmulkes game!

ALUBAT: I've got a better idea. Let's eat. We've been hiding behind that *étagère* for a millennium. I'm so hungry I could eat 24 carrots.

SCAEVOLA: You two swabbies can subsist on gruel and grits and strawberry Kool-Aid all the way to Arcturus. You will salute at the hint of my shadow, and refer to me as Admiral Scaevola. My Princess and I, on the other hand, shall feast on *chilaquiles* and *enfrijoladas,* and wash it all down with fresh *nectar de los dioses* from the *manantial del maguey.* But you may join us at the Admiral's table properly attired with towels on your arms, and swill your gruel after you have attended to our whims. Shall we dine?

ACT II --   **Scene 1. The Game Room of the spaceship. Scaevola, Alubat, and Milliwit are seated at a round table. Laya is standing to one side with an open hatbox, the contents of which are not visible. The chorus lurks.**

MILLIWIT: *(saluting and burping)* Haven't had grits as great as those since my barefoot days back in Dogpatch. By grannies, Admiral, I must admit that vittles hatched by that Philosopher's Stone *(ta-da!)* of yours are mighty toothsome.

SCAEVOLA: At ease, maggot Milliwit. Let us attend to the Princess as she explains the workings of her sainted mother's *pasatiempo.*

LAYA: Y'r attention, please, gents. In this hatbox we have a total o' five yarmulkes. Two are white, an' three are black. I'm goin' to blindfol' each o' y' an' place a yarmulke on each o' y'r r'spective noddles. Then I'll r'move th' blindfol's. Th' first one t' guess what color is his own yarmulke wins an extra helpin' o' gruel. But y'gotta come up with a reas'nable expl'nation, an' I'm th' d'cider as t' who's the best d'ducer. Me mum tells me that in her time, her daddy used t' play this game with travelin' salesmen. T' help sharpen focus, th' winners got t' kiss his dotter (me mum), an' the losers were all dunked in th' outhouse. Th' Gran' Prize went t' me daddy.

SCAEVOLA: Ha! You two losers will get double latrine duty. And I would think, Princess, that when I win I should rate at least a peck on the cheek.

CHORUS: Princess Laya winks with a *Gioconda* smile, applies the blindfolds, puts the white yarmulkes on Milliwit and Alubat, and a black one on Scaevola. She removes the blindfolds and Scaevola, seeing the two white yarmulkes, immediately begins to laugh hysterically. Beads of perspiration populate his brow. He remains immobilized by hilarity. Milliwit raises his hand.

MILLIWIT: Mine's black! I get to kiss the princess!

SCAEVOLA: What th'? No you don't. What makes you think your yarmulke is black? (*Aside*) My goodness, mercy me! My anointed head runneth over! Callooh! Callay!

MILLIWIT: My Physics teacher always said that black absorbs heat, and white reflects it. Since they installed the yarmulke on my humble crown, sweat has been pouring down my brow, as well as yours, Scroobola, I mean Admiral Scaevola of the black beanie. Alubat's brow and his immaculately white yarmulke are as dry as dry ice. Q.E.D. Computer science triumphs! Even geniuses like you can lose a few.

LAYA: Y'r Googlin' brain is cogitatin' GIGO. Jus' two maj'r points. ONE: I accident'ly got some ketchup on one o' th' yarmulkes an' jus' rins'd it off. Th' very one I put on y'r noddle. It's not sweat, it's H-two-an'-O. TWO: look at y'r beanie y'rself. It's white. Roun' two comin' up. Default points f'r Muzzie an' Asar.

MILLIWIT: *La maledizione!*

SCAEVOLA: There are only two white yarmulkes! I knew mine was black immediately! It was so obvious, it was hilarious! I could not but guffaw.

CHORUS: Princess Laya puts a white yarmulke on Scaevola, and a black one on the other two. Scaevola again is convulsed in a paroxysm of chortle. Alubat raises his hand.

ALUBAT: My yarmulke is white! The holy gruel is mine!

LAYA: F' real? How do y' figger that, o gran' Zorro o' th' Freudian fields?

ALUBAT: Skinner guides my mind. I see a white yarmulke on Admiral Scaevola. And a black yarmulke on Milliwit. If I had a white yarmulke, Milliwit would have known immediately that he had a black yarmulke, because otherwise Scaevola would have seen the only two white yarmulkes, and would have raised his hand before Milliwit could blink. But Scaevola's still adrift in chuckle, consumed with selfesteem, and Milliwit has no clue. Do you follow my logic?

SCAEVOLA: Logic worthy of a Skinnerhead, matey. Never overestimate your adversary. Inspect your beanie, you maggoty maggot. Get busy polishing the pots in the scullery, you two, and when that's done, you can lavenderize the lavatory.

LAYA: Adm'ral Scaevola wins by d'fault! Y'know how many beans make five, love! I'm so proud. Makes th' anticipatin' that much more worth th' anticipatin'! In th' meantime, here's y'r peck. (*Smaaack!)*

SCAEVOLA: I hear the Music of the Spheres in Dolby Sound! And so, to bed, for the first evening of the morning star. I, to my kingsized waterbed, my princess to her *lecho de pétalos de rosa,* and you two, when your chores are done, with the *cucarachas en el excusado.* I'll inspect first thing in the AM.

ACT II -- **Scene 2. The Game Room, next day. Scaevola, Laya, Milliwit.**

CHORUS: Alert, rested, and caffeinated after a rousing breakfast of rearranged molecules, the Exodus crew is ready to confront another day in the romantic nonstop rush to the as yet unexplored constellation of the Ploughman Boötes, the Driver of the Celestial Bears, with its shiny Bear Guard, Arcturus.

SCAEVOLA: We have an exciting activity in store. What joy and good fellowship we shall convivialate on this day! I promised you, my dear, that I would invent clever diversions to while away the eons! This is installment number two. We shall inaugurate my latest contrivance: The Future According to the Head Under the CAT. What's that? This morning I arose at dawn's crack, that is to say, I got up before any of you slugabeds. I converted my sainted mother-in-law's bonnie yarmulkes - after all, their highly entertaining purpose has been served, and to the benefit and ultimate wisdom of us all, I might add -- I converted these most edifying instruments into some very special Computerized Axial Tomographs to plug into my Eidoideator. Each of you places one on your head just like you would any ordinary yarmulke, and you then imagine what you would like to see when we finally arrive at our glorious destination, Arcturus, the Guard of the Bears. I shall afterwards delight you with a Technicolored, SurroundSound sensation as the Eidoideator generates an Oscarworthy cinematic experience - an audiovisual interpretation of your dream! It will enhance our anticipation of the day when the Bear Guard - not the Bear - is in our front yard! We shall commence just as soon as Alubat comes out of the comfort station.

ALUBAT: (*entering noisily from adjoining comfort station*) HELP! There's a MONSTER in the toilet!

CHORUS: Milliwit and Laya fearlessly rush into the comfort station to see for themselves, followed by a skeptical Scaevola. One by one they return with looks of amazement and dismay engraved on their faces.

ALUBAT: What in the blazes is it?

LAYA: A giant earwig in a space monster suit!

MILLIWIT: Looks to me like two medusas fraternizing!

SCAEVOLA: *(angrily)* Whatever it is, it's another sneaky freeloader, and I really don't need any more of those.

ALUBAT: We of the Freudian cloth joshingly call this an attentiongetting shenanigan. Actually, I pasted a Rorschach inkblot to the toilet seat to plumb your respective psyches. Your interpretations provide to me great insights into your metaphysical innards. You see, I took a class in inkblot analysis and am certified to interpret your hallucinations. You, my dear, by seeing an entity disguised as something else, are obviously harboring a dark secret. And you, colleague Milliwit, there's no question about what's on *your* perverted mind. You, Admiral Scaevola *(saluting)* with all due respect, Sir, I find you seriously disturbed. As are you all, bordering on a slide into *dementia praecox*. You see, the image was, after all, just an inkblot on a toiletseat, as any stable individual would have observed. Not to worry, however. We have time and space on our hands, and I can psychoanalyze all of you on route. We will uncover naughty little skeletons hiding within your subconscious that are making you see monsters and medusas where there are only inkblots. What better way to trundle down the eons to Arcturus! We'll all have a good laugh, and you'll be able to see inkblots instead of scary bugaboos when we're through. But that's many miles down the starpike. And I would only ask in return a less monotonous bill of fare, delicious though the actual one may be. I have with me here in my *attaché* a myriad of psychoanalytic exams that will fill your waking hours with fascinating divination into why you think what you think. Then we can discuss how you can train yourself to think something else. And after that I can devise brand new tests along the way. There's no end to psychological fun and games.

SCAEVOLA: Forgive me, my dear maggot, but the screwloose here appears to me to be you. However, your vaudeville science may indeed provide us with a few laughs along the weary way, and may some spaceday even prove to be relevant to something or another. In the meantime, I have planned our program for this day, and after all, I am the boss, and don't need any attentiongetting device to command your attention. My little skit, you will see, is a bit of a mindpicker, too, but it's based on hardrocket science. Allow me.

CHORUS: Scaevola places the hatbox of yesterday on the center of the table. He then removes from it the five ex bonnie yarmulkes. They have been upgraded to include an antenna and flashing lights. He clicks on the Eidoideator with his wizard wand, and instructs his crewpersons to each take a modified yarmulke and place it on his or her head. They uneasily but dutifully comply. Laya arises, takes one of the two remaining, and places it on the crown of spaceking Scaevola. He cannot resist her charms, shrugs, and there it sits.

LAYA: Let the games begin! You first, me amazin' lord an' master. Show us the way.

CHORUS: Scaevola bows, takes a chair, closes his eyes and smiles. Except for our soothing choral recitative, silence reigns for a good twenty seconds. Then Scaevola speaks.

SCAEVOLA: It's your turn, Milliwit. Just tune in to the infinite, as they are wont to say, and let your mind rattle around in the tin can of possibility. Snap your synapses, and generate your idealized construct of our future life in the bosom of the Bear Guard!

CHORUS: Milliwit repeats the performance of Scaevola, followed by Alubat, and finally, by Princess Laya. An eternity seems to elapse as on we drone. Ommmmmmmmmmmm.

SCAEVOLA: Now shall ye witness the marvels of genius mentation. Allow me a moment to rewind the presentation. I should tell you that my description of what you are about to see was necessarily deceptive. You will see not what your conscious mind wanted the rest of us to think you wanted to see. One at a time, we will witness what each of your subconscious minds would really like to see, and how you would like your fellowtravelers to react to it. This way we know where we stand and are off to an honest start. We'll have plenty of time to resolve any differences. Why wait until they collide before we start working on them? I myself have naught to conceal from you. You know where I stand.

CHORUS: All three crewmembers immediately try to hide behind the *étagère,* but Scaevola follows and sternly points to the game table. They meekly return. Scaevola dims the lights, and waves the remote at the Eidoideator. The first subconscious musings will be those of Dr. Scaevola himself. A color portrait of the Bridge of Light to Valhalla gradually appears as a backdrop on the stage. Downstage are **Muzio Scaevola** and *Laya. Milliwit* and *Alubat* are upstage, moving hods of bricks.

SCAEVOLA: *My dearest Princess, by virtue of my stature as Monarch of this Great Plowman Galaxy, I swap my Admiral's spyglass for Wotan's spear, and dub thee Fricka, Queen of Boötes, with your tiara of sparkling baubles, worthy of your royal gender! Hey, you Fasolt and Fafner midgets over there, keep moving and get our Valhalla pieced together, if you expect any gruel for dinner. And now, Queen Fricka, to populate this vast empire! In a generation or two we'll have filled Valhalla with fruitful progeny!*

(LAYA):   *Oh mighty Wotan, me liege an' master! I tremble with passion t' comply with y'r command, an' am prepared t' revel with you on y'r waterbed o' pleasure f'r an etern'ty, flesh with flesh t' beget flesh fr nonendin' gen'rations!*

CHORUS: Valhalla fades away, to the massive, noble sounds of the concluding chords of *Das Rheingold*. You can't tell, but Scaevola is actually blushing. Under the patina of genius, he's just another guy with gonads. Fade in to a backdrop of the greenish twilight of a watery Eden. Now it's showtime for the id of **Reddy Milliwit**. Upstage are *Scaevola*, *Laya* and *Alubat*, acting like they're swimming around. *Scaevola* has a fannypack that every few seconds emits an audible *ta-da!*, leading us to conclude that it holds the Philosopher's Stone (*ta-da!*), which made this entire episode possible. **Milliwit** enters downstage stealthily, glancing nervously about, broadcasting evil intent. He switches to a smiley face, and swims toward the frolicking group. Suddenly he snatches the fannypack from the disarmed *Scaevola*, and swims away, laughing raucously. In **Milliwit**'s perverse imagination, the balance of power has tilted to the dark side.

MILLIWIT: *Now you can get to work, Scaevola! You and Alubat will make a good team of grunts to finish up the Valhalla project! Princess, swim away with me! Not only do I have the power, I have the prowess!*

(LAYA): *You were always the one I lusted f'r, Reddy me prince! Y'know what I'm sayin'? S' long, losers!*

CHORUS: Remember, dear audience, these are only the wishfulthink projections of each individual crew member, made available for public viewing one at a time by Scaevola's infernal machine. *The words attributed to the others are only what each crew member would like them to be.* But what the blazes could Scaevola have been thinking to come up with this in the first place? Their spacetrail relationships may never be the same again. Accompanied by the swirling music that concludes the first scene of *Das Rheingold*, the Rhine sequence fades and the thoughts of **Asar Alubat** invade the stage. We now see a backdrop of a giant Rorschach inkblot. Background music from *L'Enfant et les Sortilèges*. *Scaevola* and *Milliwit*, in horrible Hallowe'en masks, are upstage, gesticulating like Sendak monsters. A frightened **Alubat** is downstage.

ALUBAT: *¡Mamá! ¡Mamá! Save me from the spacemonsters!*

(LAYA): *(appearing from stage right) Come t' me arms, me beamish boy! I mus' exorcise those wicked images!*

ALUBAT: *Yes, mamá, spank me, spank me!*

CHORUS: She puts **Alubat** on her lap, unbelts his pants, and proceeds to spank him as he squeals with pleasure. The upstage monsters disappear. The scene fades to the final strains of *L'Enfant et les Sortilèges*. NOW whose face is red? But it's **Princess Laya**'s turn to broadcast her deepest thoughts and hopes. Music from *The Drunken Concubine* fills the game room. On the backdrop appear simply the masks of Thalia and Malpomene. **Laya** is alone, downstage.

LAYA: *It's show an' tell time; like, it's a f'real deal from here on in. How do I break th' news to this guy? Like I yam what I yam an' that's all that I yam! An' I know what I'm sayin'.*

(SCAEVOLA): *(bounding in from the wings) What are you saying, my Princess of the Latest Generation? We have arrived at the Eden of Arcturus; we are prepared to create the future!*

LAYA: *Good, foolish, genius shipmate, I'm not what I appear t' be. I was not, as advertised to you, the star o' Pinocchio's o' Pleasure Island. I was in fac' the star o' Finoccio's o' North Beach! I'm a guy in drag. Y' have no idea how weary, stale an' flat, albeit profit'ble, is life in drag on stage! I longed to get away from it all. But it was never a to-be-or-not situation. At night, on Mt. Davidson, I use' t' implore th' gods o' th' fog f'r a shot at more challengin' profession an' a bran' new venue! When I emailed y' me allurin' photo on th' Playface.com chatroom, y' presented me with an option for a new, excitin' life, an' I grabbed it. Y' tol' me o' your infatuation with th' Mixtec maidens o' Oaxaca* as y'r ideal madres o' mañana, an' y'r failure to recruit even una f'r y'r gran' endeavor. So I was only y'r runnerup, y'r worse-is-nothin'. But like I saw this one comin', lovie! I picked up a doz'n frozen eggs at th' blackmarket in th' Walmart parkin' lot, an' f'r a pittance was able t' snag on eBay a Gladbag full o' toenail clippin's from th' Mayday Queen o' Nochixtlán! Like it's a gif' from gratef'l me t' gen'rous you. Muzzie, y' can clone an' incubate all th' progeny y' need with th' DNA y' got in this Gladbag!

(SCAEVOLA): ¡Ay caramba! Now it's my turn in the confessional. I read you as a ladyboy from day one. But now hear my story. I was the only child of Lord and Lady Sluice, of Emerald City peerage. My name at birth was not Muzio Scaevola, but Ozma Ova Sluice, an anagramatically correct name befitting my rank and gender. During the Revolution, my parents were beheaded, and my nanny whisked me away to Sardinia, where I was raised by my Aunt Mombi Scaevola. To protect me from Sinn Féin spies, she dressed me as a boy and dubbed me Muzio Scaevola. Suspecting that a career as boy genius at that time would be more politically correct than one as girl genius, I stayed in boymode. We won't need any blackmarket eggs. But it was a noble gesture.

CHORUS: The images fade away to the final strains of Act II Scene 1 of *Fidelio*. The joy of Beethoven is not echoed in the faces of those seated at the game table in the spacecraft *Exodus*. The Future According to the Head Under the CAT has bombed.

ACT III --   **Control Room of the *Exodus*. It is empty. A computer desktop at the control panel is trumpeting *reveille*.**

CHORUS: 150 million years have passed since Scaevola's id animator ruined the rest of the trip for all concerned. Some thoughts and speculations are probably better left repressed, at least in public. After that debacle, Scaevola set the spacecraft on autopilot, and all retired to the Absolutely Cold Pantry, each encasing himself in a cryofridge box, awaiting a better day, when *Exodus* will be reborn as *Genesis* and they arrive at the neighborhood of the Bear Guard. The computer wakeup alarm was set to blare on that very day. Suddenly a rasping noise invades the melody of reveille. Look! The pantry door is slowly creaking open! Scaevola, Milliwit, Alubat, and Laya emerge. Scratching and yawning, they nonetheless appear not a day older, but like wine past its prime, all are less appealing. Scaevola runs to the control panel, views the desktop screen, shuts off the alarm, and, consternated, slaps his forehead.

SCAEVOLA: *¡Ay caramba!* Why have so many years passed us by? Traveling at a cautious 60% lightspeed, we should have gotten here in 60 years. But this is ridiculous! And of all schemes o' mighty men, this was the best laid. This is an intergalactic goof! Enlighten me, my son, my wise Computer Program!

COMPUTER: We kept running into those damned plasmons on the way, o loin of my creation. It looks like a straight shot to Arcturus but it's not, not by a very long shot. We had to go light years around a bunch of humongous invisible bodies to stay on track. Those plasmonic screens are actually hiding secret universes. This is pushing my gazilllibyte capacity, but I think that once there we ran into a dimensional hole. I mean we could see Arcturus bright and clear, but no way could we get through that hole. We had to go around it, and that trek itself was good for a good 60 million years. Can you believe that? No way is anything a straight shot out here. I did the best I could, dad.

SCAEVOLA: (*peering out the ethershield window*) Alas, so bugbogged down in Ptolomeic perspective we are oblivious to the vast vistas of neo astronomy! But if we're here now, where is Arcturus? All I spot is a big, black *nada*.

CHORUS: The others, their embarrassment cobwebbed by 150 million years, gather around the ethershield. They, too, are visibly agitated. Alubat, obsessed with the notion of coming up with a catchphrase akin to "...a giant pratfall for mankind," picks up the wizard wand and sneaks into the Game Room. The voice of Alubat fulminates:

(VOICE OF ALUBAT): ***"Drifting worlds impotent with age, Universes weary of cataclysm and fire, Dimming stars and cooling suns, Your jaded gods dream of dreaming other games..."***

THE END *Is Near!*

MILLIWIT: We hitched a ride on a tedious trek to this turkeyhole in the sky? Even your *ta-da* petrock can't alakazam full out of empty. I'll wager that Devil's Island boasts superior appointment. What! No exit from the *Exodus*? And we endured an eon of claustrophobia to end up stuck here for an infinity encore? I need no Eidoideator to announce that *the bridge to the future is in the cards*. Get back in here, Alubat. First on the agenda: let's teach the Admiral how to play a bracing game of Fiftytwo Pickup.

LAYA: Look over there! Is that a floater in me eyeball or is that a glimmer I'm spottin'?

SCAEVOLA: *Sí, sí,* Princeperson Laya! I keep forgetting that an eon or two has flown by. Enough time has elapsed for Arcturus to collapse into a white dwarf! But it's still got plenty of stuff inside, and I can fashion a planet or two with it and still leave us with a shiny heater in the sky! We'll just have to mosey up a bit closer, and I'll polish up my Philosopher's Stone (*ta-da!*), roll up my sleeves, and get to work! My dear sir, sir but dear nonetheless, we indeed could use those ova and that Gladbag of toenail clippings. We'll clone us some merry Mixtec maidens in the lab and alakazam up a race of winners! And we'll need our competing and contrasting DNA's to survive in this madcap universe!

COMPUTER: If I may, dad. You've got a good track record at putting together some mighty convincing androids. You might consider carrying it one step further and transferring your mind systems to some robot lookalikes and discarding those messy organic shells. Your Stone (*ta-da!*) can supply you with any exotic elements you may require in the manufacturing process. If anyone can pull it off, you can, sire. Just a thought. Bounce it around with the boys.

SCAEVOLA: Hmmmm. By Jove, I never thought of that. *¡Ay chihuahua!* Me motley mateys, we're on the verge of something REALLY BIG!

CHORUS: Alubat has paid no attention to the pleas of his colleague and is seen through the paneless window waving the wand at the Eidoideator again. As the penultimate strains of *Night on Bald Mountain* sound in the background, the players freeze in position as the voice of Asar Alubat fulminates:

(VOICE OF ALUBAT): ***"Out of whose womb came the ice? And the hoary frost of heaven, who hath gendered it? Canst*** *thou bring forth Mazzaroth in his season? or canst thou guide Arcturus with his sons? Knowest thou the ordinances of heaven? ... If there be any virtue, and if there be any praise, think on these things."*

CHORUS: Princeperson Laya suddenly unfreezes and races into the game room. She/he moves toward the unseen Eidoideator and stops in the middle of the paneless window. She/he is seen to hurl some projectile at the infernal machine and a crash is heard. The strains of *Night on Bald Mountain* wind down like a decelerating turntable. Laya turns to face the others in the Control Room.

LAYA: Lovie, this m'chine o' y'rs is jus' trouble an' a half. Like, it's th' voice o' th' divil hisself. Don' be mesm'rized by that crazy id o' Alubat, or me own f'r that matter. This is no time f'r th' mas'chistic el'quence o' ol' man Job an' 'is 'mag'nary ord'nances. Take a hike, Mazz'roth, you an' y'r silly season. Hifalutin Palaver is jus' another brand o' MaryJane. Th' party's kaput, gents, an' it's grunt an' sweat time f'r all o' us. An' th' ta-da rock is pretty amazin', but, like, it's no Magic Belt o' Ozma. Y' know what I'm sayin'? It'll conj'r up the Legos, but we gotta stick 'em together on our own time. Cheer up, me bitchin' biddies! We've still got our Heads, our Hearts, our Hands an' our Health! An' like we got Muzzie here t' enhance all Four o' them Aitches! An' yessiree, we'll ride herd on ol' pooped-out Arcturus an' 'is do-nothin' sons. We got th' rhythm an' we got th' jazz t' bring forth a merry worl' o' pretty smarties!

CHORUS: Scaevola and Milliwit cry "Hear hear!" and "Huzzah!" as Laya enters triumphantly into the Control Room. A humbler, disenthralled Alubat, evangelized by Laya's hortatory exuberance, follows her/him and joins the celebration. They hoist Laya onto their shoulders and march off the stage as the computer cheers. The stage darkens, and as the curtain falls, an inspired orchestra plays the final bars of the Introduction to – what else? - *Also Sprach Zarathustra*. But the final words are ours:

THE END

and begin again

Mr. Vici Forges a Coalition

When vital interests are at stake, peaceful solutions are feasible when each side feels that synergy is at work. This is always possible, and successful negotiation is not a zero sum game. The following declamatory conversation may or may not chronicle one of these occasions. It is yet another saga of a war of the worlds, but negotiation does turn out to be a viable option. In a galactic game of civilized confrontation, earth is pitted against a longdistance planet billions and billions and billions of miles from earth's polluted shores, populated by inorganic ascetics. Who's the winner? It all depends on what you mean.

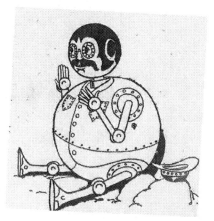

MR. VICI FORGES A COALITION

ACT I: The constellation of Pegasus, on the planet Fiftyone Pegasi, in the plainjane metropolis of Theodoricburg, hub of Astrogoth civilization. Within the frugal Board Room of the Astrogoth Brotherhood is the Plutonian emissary Capt. Gundar, and the image of Chairman Joseph, who appears as a giant head plugged into the wall.

CHORUS: Captain Gundar, presently nuncio plenipotentiary of Mr. Vici, *mandamás* of the dwarfplanet Pluto, is meeting with the Chairman of the Astrogoth Brethren in order to further advance a vast galactic conspiracy. Mr. Vici himself is a bulky mindmass lodged in the Plutonian substrata.

DRAMATIS PERSONAE:

CAPTAIN GUNDAR	PRAGMATIST
CHAIRMAN JOSEPH	ANDROID CHAIRMAN
EVA SNARCESOR	ADMIRAL
ATOM SNURL	AMORAL CAPTAIN
GUS GRUNCH	PROLETARIAN
CRAL CAVINU	SELFMADE ROBOT
GONERIL O'NUKER	BUGBOG TOPDOG
JACKARMSTRONG CLUSTER	BRASS GOFER
ADMIRAL BARSOOM	CONSIGLIERE
MR. VICI	BEAUTIFUL MIND
BILLY BRUTUS	INTERROGATOR
MRS. DEFARGE	NEIGHBORHOOD WATCHER
CHORUS	ENTERTAINERS

While Mr. Vici is ambitiously interested in figuring out the universe, Joseph and his brothers are committed to the advancement of Astroascetism. Pluto and Fiftyone Pegasi are temporarily allied in stamping out an insidious virus emanating from the planet bugbog. Captain Gundar, a bugbog turncoat, is the pawn of Mr. Vici, who must rely on mobile mortal instruments to advance his galactic interests.

GUNDAR: Greetings, august Chairman Joseph of the Astrogoth Brotherhood. At last we meet! I bring you tidings from Mr. Vici, Pretender to the Summit of Wisdom. He has prepared for you "Bugbog Rocket Science for the Astroascetically Minded," an exhaustively researched manual of operation for the bugbog spaceships that he commandeered and teletransported to you from Pluto, so you can operate them on their own power. This handsome tome has been delivered, with due pomp, to your designated underlings. Presto digitato! The sudden menacing appearance on bugbog of the entire VENI fleet, long believed crashed beyond recognition on a hostile Plutonian plain, will shock, awe, and terrorize bugbog into submission! Excuse me, but am I addressing a computer?

JOSEPH: We have evolved into bionic beings and are ourselves the children of our future. Longer shelf life, my dear artifact of auld lang syne. Our misanthropologists have analyzed bugbog evolution and concluded that bugboggers are bumpkin cousins indeed, challenged as they are in spatial imagination. Beings of more efficient construct on other planets in your puny solar system successfully migrated to more upscale neighborhoods eons ago, taking with them every vestige of their scrubby solar existence. Only bugboggers remained stuck in their mud, seeing other planets as empty real estate and assuming that the bugbog life system as intelligently designed by Yaweh the Great and Terrible defined "life" for the entire universe. In the meantime they messed up their own planet due to congenital tunnelvision. Pleasure for organic beings consists primarily in relief from built-in or self-inflicted unpleasantness. Bugbog technological advances have ever been dedicated to the slaughter and occasional consumption of all other life forms, and to the devising of infernal mechanisms for self immolation. This suicidal myopia was of little interest to us until now. Bugboggers have irresponsibly permitted a deadly computer virus to metastasize and menace the very existence of Computer Assisted Life As We Know It. We can afford to ignore them no longer, and will attempt to educate the bugbog race of miniminds into undoing the cosmic errors of their ways. My underlings have drawn up lesson plans. But just what is your interest in this matter? You are a bugbogger yourself. Why do you militate in the ranks of Vici against your own ilk? Explain!

GUNDAR: Thrilled to the bonematter that you should ask, most wily Chairman of Board. One virtue of my otherwise viceridden race is the ability of many of us to adapt to prevailing winds of opportunity. Not all of us are mired in smothering dogma. Some of us can actually divine on which side our bread is buttered. We on bugbog are surrounded by aments who would risk the future of all of us for the promises of phantoms they observe up their own fundament. *Chusma* bugboggers are facile to gull, and unprincipled manipulators play games marching *chusma* over cliffs. As a selfserving realist, I prefer to simply defect. Let them eat *caca!*

JOSEPH: I read you. Anyway, the enemy of my enemy is still the enemy of my enemy, or he was the last time I checked it out. We can work together during that moment of stasis. Then too, the enemy of my enemy may be a small potato enemy to him, but a hot potato enemy to me. That can change the equation. We'd better monitor the relationship all the time. Meanwhile, let us concentrate on defusing bugbog malediction. Thanks for the manual of operation but what does your devious boss, Mr. Vici, expect to get out of our collaboration? This was never really spelled out, either. Organic mass that he is, no computer virus can affect him. On the other hand, with just a whiff of meningococci, his foolish practice of unprotected cerebrophagy could lead to a "Vale, Vici" scenario before you could mutter, for example, "spinal tap."

GUNDAR: My boss is very brainy. He has barrels of antibiotics and vaccines stored away for any such emergency. But he also understands that the spread of a bugbog computer virus throughout the universe would obliterate great bionic civilizations in one dominowave, and he would be left with fewer blossoms of knowledge to gather on route to the

Summit of Wisdom. This is his announced agenda. He requests only that following Victory-Over-Bugbog Day you send your best minds to Pluto for a thoughtsharing convention on the Meaning of Consciousness. That is his area of concern.

JOSEPH: Mr. Vici himself sounds like a figment from somebody's fundament. However, attending a boring convention is a pittance to pay for an enterprise of such pith as this. I must remind you that you have delivered but four of the five Victorious Spaceships of the bugbog fleet promised us. You must of course teletransport the fifth Victorious Ship to us pretty soon, or the deal is off, and we'll proceed to Plan B. Please explain this to Mr. Hermitcrab Vici. The contingency being that your manual of operation actually can explain how to get these bugbog birds to fly. Our best megaminds have not been able to crack the secret maneuver. Could it be that we were looking for sophistication in a problem framed by sillybillies? Our brief conversation makes me wonder. You might tell him that we can look into encoding all of the data in his burgeoning memorybank on the point of a pin and transfer his mind to something mobile and certainly more secure than its present venue, if he's interested. It could be to our mutual advantage. And maybe you'd be interested in a hardy tincan epidermis yourself. We could translate you into an Astrogoth RoboGundar in a NewYorkjiff.

GUNDAR: You may not believe this, but that's an option that never occurred to me in all my moments of wildancrazy. Tell me do, what do you guys do all day, anyway? What keeps you perkin'? And if our organic pleasure is only a brief respite from unpleasantry, at least the net result is still pleasantry. Where do you guys go to for that?

JOSEPH: Spoken like the bugbog Babbitt that you really are. The idea that another life form could exist apart from your own race of inbred Narcissies is so alien to you that you cannot fathom what it implies. Why, even your Great and Terrible Yaweh looks and acts just like you. As to our pastimes, we do play our robogames when we're not on the job. And we do derive satisfaction in observing that our advances in knowledge and technique are fruitful. We spend our time working toward those ends, and a hefty chunk of it is devoted to providing sources of energy and maintenance to meet our physical requirements, just as you do. But this, too, takes on a different expression from that of your bugbog activity. You might find it ironic to note that alcohol is one of our alternative sources of energy, and we devote considerable effort toward its production and distribution. Anyway, my offer stands. Mull it over in your dreams.

GUNDAR: As to your offer, I'll so mull and inform my boss. As to your other concerns, you do entertain me with your Astrogoth banter, ho ho! But in no way, *Don José*, can it fail, our Plan A! Put your circuits to rest on all accounts. It is true that (one): their fifth spaceship got away from us temporarily. However, we have learned that it was forced to land on our own tiny satellite Nyx. A contingent of mortal instruments is on route at this moment to bring these addlepates to justice, and teletransport the Victorious bugbog vessel to your domain. And (two): Not to worry. The trick for startup involves stepping on the clutch. Clearly spelled out in our lavishly illustrated manual of operation. As to the specifics of our mutual defense agreement, we have prepared it for you in duplicate. Look it over at your leisure, and tomorrow I'll be off with a signed copy for Mr. Vici. You'll find no surprises, just a formal declaration of what we've already agreed upon. Where's my room? Unlike you roboSpartans, I need to grab some shuteye before the long trek tomorrow.

JOSEPH: My legal advisors will check out your document. In the meantime, you can sleep on the floor in the broom closet over there. You'll find it inordinately clean, but nothing fancy. No frills on Fiftyone Pegasi. For your organic needs, you'll find a waste disintegrator in the corner and a keg of H_2O on the shelf. Goodnight.

GUNDAR: Holy smoke! Vici will fork over combat pay for this gig.

CHORUS: A screensaver appears on computer screen. Gundar walks over to the designated door. As he opens the door, he turns off the lights in the throne room. A closing door is heard, and the only thing visible on stage is the screensaver, as the curtain falls on Act I.

ACT II: **Scene 1. The satellite Nyx, tiny rockmoon of miniPluto. Admiral Snarcesor, Capt. Snurl, and Petty Officer "Pegleg" Grunch are huddled around a campfire. The Victorious Ship Excelsior is seen upstage.**

CHORUS: Spacefleet Admiral Eva Snarcesor and her fiancé Capt. Atom Snurl, along with Petty O. "Pegleg" Grunch, have escaped with the spaceworthy Excelsior from Mr. Vici, godfather and spiritual mentor of the dwarf planet Pluto. However, they were unable to make the great leap in their endeavor to return to their bugbog planet home. Initially impressive in their daring repo operation, in their desperation to succeed they did not notice the minimoon Nyx in their path, and although clever maneuvering by Capt. Snurl saved them from collision, they were forced to land upon tiny Nyx. Having used up all of their reserve fuel in the takeoff from Pluto and the subsequent braking and landing maneuvers on Nyx, they find themselves again stranded in hostile territory. They realize that Vici's minions will soon overtake and subject them to horrors better left undescribed.

EVA: O me o my! What a mess I mus' confess! Fetch us some rocket fuel, Snurl you darlin' fool. T' take care o' th' details, on Cap'ns, Admir'ls depen'. Get us outa here, or on th' yardarm you'll be sportin' a necktie, me love. Now that's a resultgettin' line.

SNURL: Well, bow wow wow, ma bonny bit bairnie. But no fangs in thy bark do I perceive; in thy posturin' there is a gap of credibility. No matter. I wink and salute. Let us explore this barren stone and exact victory from its bowels. Something combustible enough to free us from the gravity of this puny planetary system we may find. *Gravity is law and relativity is theory, yet gravity is relative. Parse <u>that</u>, O Porter G. Perrin!*

GRUNCH: Avast, Cap'n, sir! You give our Admiral no respect! Just you wait until Commissioner O'Nuker hears about your disrespectful insubordination! With all due respect, I speak my humble piece, sir.

SNURL: Of reason, lowly Petty-O, are you bereft? Not to the exalted Admiral Snarcesor, but to me, you report. One more piece like that one, and for uppity sass detrimental to military tradition I'll write you up! What's more, when mentioning Commissioner Goneril O'Nuker's name, you genuflect! *To crush the coolies, rattle the chains of command.*

EVA: Bad Cap'n Snurl. Sit! Stay! Who's in charge here? Leave Petty-O Grunch t'me. Y'r demoralizin' th' crew.

SNURL: Ma sonsie hiney, whit come o' oor haund-astin, Eva Snarcesor, ma jo? *A cocked hat ill sits on an airhead.*

EVA: Remember y'r lieut's roots, Cap'n Snurl. I made y' a cap'n an' if I've a min' I can make y' a lowly seaman soon enough, an' it's reportin' y'll be in steerage t' Petty-O Grunch! Respec' mus' be paid!

SNURL: P-O Grunch, my insolent man, see what unrest you wreak? For the nonce you'd best hobble over to an asteroid pockmark within hailing distance, and invisible-ize yourself. When you're required, the tocsin will knell. Beyond your unwashed earshot the Admiral and I have officious business to discuss. Begone! *A taste o' the cat would remind 'im where 'e's at.*

EVA: Oh Atom, me virile male cap'n! Didn' y' unnerstan' th' li'l admiralizin' I had t' put on f'r P-O Grunch! He's the only crew we got, an' words, like flags an' medals an' ep'lets, buy alot o' loy'lty, lovey.

SNURL: So thou, for the swabbie, was't but putting on a show! Happy days again are here! But awastin' is time, lassie o' mine! Hark! I do hear, in mine own little ear, Vici's chariot hurrying near, by mindless mortal instruments manned! On the way they are, *Excelsior* to recapture, and us to deliver to oblivion. Together with Grunch the grunt, kindling let us gather for blastoff to our planet of earth! Let sound the tocsin! Recall P-O Grunch! *Man who waits for time is booby.*

EVA: Overcomin' is our destiny! Off we go inta th' frost o' Nyx t' pick up sticks! Ding dong, ding dong!

CHORUS: The tocsin has knelled. P-O Grunch reappears and stands at attention as strains of Souza seem to fill the frigid air. In venerable Suribachi posture, VENI's hardscrabble crew on the outpost at the edge of eternity unfurls the bugbog standard. Mindful of time constraint, the troupe marches forward in doubletime to tame the pygmy satellite and rob it of its combustibles.

ACT II: **Scene 2. Down the rocky road a piece. Upstage looms an unexpected igloo.**

CHORUS: The plucky trio in ten minutes or so has marched halfway around the puny moon. Doubletime is particularly a challenge to old "Pegleg," but he revels in affliction. So far their quest to amass anything which could ignite a blastoff has been a bust. But failure daunts them only a little bit. The sudden appearance of an igloo on the landscape has aroused their curiosity. Commodore Cral Cavinu resides within. Who is Cavinu? You'll see if you bide a wee.

EVA: Oh my oh me! Unalone are we, on the desert of adversity! Advance, P-Officer Grunch, and greet warmly any den'zen of Nyx that inside may reside!

SNURL: Indeed. This foeman, to the lay of the land of Nyx is privy! Social banter is inappropriate. If we subject him to interrogation, perhaps he will his guts spill, and re our exit from Nyx tell us how that bill to fill!

Do your dirtywork, P-O Grunch. Keelhaul the landlubber! *For the quick fix, skip the carrots for the sticks.*

EVA: Are y' nane s' weel furnish'd i' th' haid, or what, Cap'n Rummydummy? How can y' assume (one) the den'zen can unnerstan' wha' y'r askin' 'im (two) he knows th' ans'r or (three) he wouldn' be happy to share it with y' anyway f'r his own reas'ns? Quit y'r male bumblin' an' watch how a lady earns her admir'l paycheck! Knock p'litely on th' igloo door, P-O, an' when it op'ns, sing th' den'zen a verse from "It's a Small Worl' After All." If that don't melt his col' Nygian heart, nothin' will.

GRUNCH: Knock knock!

CAVINU: Who's there?

GRUNCH: Orpheus.

CAVINU: Orpheus who?

GRUNCH: Orpheus a hot cuppa coffee. *There is just one moon and one golden sun, and a smile means friendship to ev'ryone,* tra la la, la la la, tra la la, la la la, tra la la, la la la la!

CHORUS: The icedoor of the igloo opens, and a robocreature with a cocked hat peers out. Minus the headgear, he resembles that huggable copperman Tik-Tok of Oz.

CAVINU: O redletter day! You have come to rescue me at long last! I've about had it with this lousy weather.

The farther away you get from old terra, the better old terra looks. Like, you can't see the warts from here. *O earth is the planet I aspire to go, and each time that I think it, I love it mo', tra la la, la la la, tra la la, la la la, tra la la, la la la la!* I recognize your uniforms. I knew that the topbrass at our Victorious Emigration Navigation Institute would spend sleepless eons searching for me! That's what kept me going.

SNURL: A cheapo Tin Woodman like you, why would VENI pursue? Anyway, you are who, and what here do you do? Do you expect us to believe you were once a Capt. Nick Chopper in the VENI? Be wary, my ear! *The more plausible the explanation, the more probable the lie.*

CAVINU: What? You know me not? Then behold before your astounded eyes Commodore Cral Cavinu, Cap'n of the Victorious Ship *Lightnin' Bug,* with adjunct appointment to captaincy of the Victorious Ship *Top-Speed,* after it blipped off the screen. But I see I have a saga to spin for you. Pray take your boots off and enter my humble igloo. Apologies are in order, but from you to me, as you will see. Hark to my tale of hardluck. I was born in Livermore, California. As an only child, I enrolled at an early age in the Secret Squadron.

SNURL: Pardon me, o clanking satire of a commodore. On any reflecting surface have you of late your likeness glommed? To the chase, cut! To the inglorious crash on Pluto of the Victorious Ship *Lightnin' Bug,* fastforward, if indeed ever you were there. That you still live the tale to tell, how convenient! Of Mr.

Vici are you perchance a secret agent? *Starting from the beginning sets the stage for elaborate irrelevance.*

EVA: You'd bes' be quiet already, Cap'n Snurl, an' listen t' what this Com'dore den'zen has t' say. He may well be what he preten's t' be. Please tell us y'r tale o' woe, me man. If I'm a bit patronizin', it's 'cause I'm an adm'ral, an' it's m' job. But we'd really 'preciate a bit o' brev'ty.

CAVINU: Very good, Admiral, ma'am. Our good ship *Lightnin' Bug* was diverted to Pluto by nefarious device of the brainy but soulless Mr. Vici. We did not crash, but were rendered harmless by Plutonian happy gas. As Vici's mortal instrument henchthings were converging on us to commandeer our ship, I was able to snap out of induced euphoria, fire up the old bug and foil the hapless minions. And wouldn't you know? We were popping the corks and didn't notice this puny satellite until WHAMBANG! time. But our feisty bug's epitaph was yet to be writ. My uncanny response time again buffered the menacing situation, and we suffered only minor fenderbender lesions. Of course I give almighty Zeus – he is great! – credit where credit is due.

SNURL: Would that you had written down and published this experience! Who are ignorant of the past, condemned to repeat it are! And the first one to note this I'm not! Here repeating it anyway I am! *Coincidence is a warp in the woof of Intelligent Design.*

CAVINU: Anyway, as the only subscriber to Popular Mechanics aboard, I was the default fixerupper, and was attending to the nuts and bolts in preparation for another takeoff before Vici's instruments arrived. Suddenly I chanced to overhear my crew engaged in loud mutinous conversation as, to keep warm, they were polishing off our supply of Dom Perignon. They had determined that the available fuel would not even suffice to catapult *Lightnin' Bug* all the way back to earthplanet, unless some unnecessary weight were dumped. Being of portly constitution, appropriate to commodore status, I was to be their sacrificial fatgoat! They had already seized the contents of the ship's armory, and did a lousy job of concealing them under their picnic table. In any event, they were ready to uprise, just waiting for me to wrap up the repair job. My only advantage was their ignorance of my knowledge of their plot. I seized the moment and announced that I had to go to the bathroom. The fools suspected nothing. I boarded the ship, but the bathroom being just a ploy, I went immediately to the control room, only to find that the blighters had removed the keys from the ignition! I was resigned to life on this miserable satellite, but it occurred to me to toss some supplies out the window on the opposite side of *Lightnin' Bug*, including the computer repair kit and enough blocks of their solid acetylene fuel to keep me warm for an eon. The bastards had locked the larder and I couldn't get at the supply of granola bars and jerky, so I was on my own devices to forage on Nyx for sustenance. I slipped on the emergency zap-proof vest that I had tucked away under my Commodore's chair, and paused long enough to *reset their compass 180 degrees*, haha!

Back to Pluto they'll go, hohoho! On leaving my beloved bug, I told the tipsy connivers that all systems were go, and further that the chariots of Vici were hot upon us. They brandished their ordnance and coolly lased a lethal volley of zaps in my direction. I feigned consternation, ejaculated a hearty "Aargh!" and executed a convincing pratfall. I then watched as they boarded *Lightnin' Bug*, leaving me for fried on the plains of Nyx. They then shot right back to Pluto before they knew it, where I presume the mortal instruments seized them, along with my unfortunate Victorious Ship.

SNURL: That's a mighty feisty anecdote, comrade. *In a mighty mysterious way moves Zeus, by the way, but praise him anyway, hey hey!*

CAVINU: There's precious little left to relate, It didn't take long to reconnoiter the entire orb and discover that neither flora nor fauna were in evidence. To survive, I'd have to reinvent myself. So after building my igloo with some of the acetylene blocks, from the spare computer parts I put together relays and vacuum tubes and solar cells to fashion the mobile robot you see before your eyes. It only remained for me to download into its memory bank the mind of the commodore, which, egged on by necessity, I finally accomplished, just as my oxy-pac was about to run out. The trick is in the transition, by the way. The transfer itself is a pedestrian task. Zeus is great! I built myself to last at least an eon, in any case longer than my bloody flesh could have possibly endured. Neither on oxygen nor organic sustenance am I dependent, nor do I consume expensive energy for warmth. To keep me percolating, stellar radiation suffices. And I have been able to think alot and perform mental gymnastics that you wouldn't believe. My imagination was my world! Inside I'm the same old Commodore Cavinu that your forebears knew and loved, but with enhancements. And I can cavort with my grandchildren's grandchildren! Just get to know me! I did assemble a spacegram transmitter and attempted to send a message to the VENI telling them of my betrayal and exile here on Nyx, but it didn't fly. Nyx obviously sports one of these black holes at its core that gobbles up radio waves. Another one of Zeus's little jokes, hallowed be his name. That's my story, and to it I stick like Quinn.

EVA: Cavinu, y've won me over! Tears like totally fill me eyes when I think o' y'r lonely days an' nights on this forsaken real 'state! Even Zeus hisself, praise 'is name, let y' down, m'lad. Y'r a credit t' th' Institute.

SNURL: Commodore, an alliance let us forge! Even as we speak, we are in the same situation that you were generations ago! Vici's mortal instruments are on the way to damn us all to the gray plains of Asphodel! Lend us your cool retro transmitter, and I'll sprinkle it with new technology and get off a spacegram to earthplanet after liftoff, just as soon as we're out of the reach of that damned black hole. And if we can lade your acetylene blocks at once, we're all outa here, good buddy! To lose, there's no time! *In a twinkle, an exadversary is cloaked in camaraderie. And viceversary.*

CAVINU: May Zeus kiss your foot! You have delivered me from eternal imagination! Yes, yes, you may dismantle the igloo and load the acetylene blocks. There's a few more stacked outside. And the computer kit is yours. Go team! Aquarius is upon us. The cock has crowed and the dawn is broken!

SNURL: Get moving, Grunch! Dismantle and haul these blocks to our Victorious Ship *Excelsior.* To spare, we've not a nanosecond! Commodore Cavinu, sir, you may want to prepare your valise for the long trek, while, with your permission, Admiral Snarcesor and I strategize. *Let's do the plot twist.*

EVA: How's that f'r adm'ral class manipulatin', me cap'n an' cohost? Y' don' allus need t' lead w' y'r aces, me hearty! An' th' poor, tired wretch'll be a good conv'rsation piece t' 'muse us on th' trip home.

SNURL: My dearest admiral, at more than what's proper even for a fat commodore that pile of senescent junk tips the scale! Why, we'd endanger the life of our loyal crew if we took a chance with him. Holy Jehosaphat, he'd be regaling us with windy stories about his exploits in the Secret Squadron. Shot is his wad. He just doesn't fit the officer image we want the crew to look up to. And by his own account, to mutiny his lax discipline led! Eva, Eva, I've been thinking, with our surplus of fuel and no excess blubber to tote around, we'll have time to amble by Arcturus on a leisurely honeymoon cruise! In no time, a transmitter I'll rig up. And to our Victorious Emigration Navigation Institute HQ a spacegram I'll shoot off, detailing our adventures, just as soon as the acetylene to our Victorious Ship the power restores! *Your tired, your poor, your wretched make me sick.*

EVA: Y' put things inta p'rspective, sweetie! It's in his own bes' int'res'. He wooden fit in, he'd be mis'rable on earthplanet. Here he c'n p'rform his merry mental g'mnastics f'r eons. It's like totally a part of Zeus' plan, me love! We can't mess w' th' will o' Zeus.

SNURL: Eventually, he'll see that this is his home. No need to tell him now. He'll get the picture, and feel eternally in our debt. Let's hustle on back to Excelsior and alakazam! Grunch has loaded the last acetylene block, an' we're ready t' rock! *When the moon is in the Seventh House, just beat it.*

CHORUS: They drag the exhausted Grunch aboard and blast off. Commodore Cavinu, packing his bag, senses the noise and looks up in time to see *Excelsior* melting into the horizon. "*Déjà vu!*" he mutters, but no one hears. He looks like he just might look forward to the arrival of the mortal instruments.

ACT III: Scene 1. The planet bugbog. In the Great War Room of the Victorious Emigration Navigation Institute (VENI), Commissioner Goneril O'Nuker is berating Admiral Barsoom, her aide-de-camp. Lt. Col. Jack Armstrong Cluster, liaison to the Victorious Information

Decipherers Institute (VIDI), is waiting in the wings.

O'NUKER: Your entire program of Emigration Navigation is in disarray! Not one of your launches has made it out of our own solar system. You are a sillybilly. You have made me the laughingstock of Commissar Atli! I have a hard time looking him in the eye. Now, either up you'll shape or out you'll ship. I literally can't afford to give you many more chances. Atli's stockholders on the Economic Community Commissariat have been looking for results for three generations! And they fund our paychecks. And every summer seems warmer and longer. Give me some talking points on your new Victorious project that I can sell to this understandably disgruntled bunch, or we're both end up selling bananas on the street. You may come in now, Colonel Cluster.

CLUSTER: Hot news off the wireless, ma'am! Over at VIDI they have just intercepted a spacegram from the Plutonian orbit area sent to you by someone claiming to be Admiral Snarcesor, of the Victorious Ship *Excelsior*. It appears to be authentic. She has transmitted the secret handshake. Read it, Commissioner, ma'am. It'll pop y'r eyeballs.

O'NUKER: What th'! This changes everything! A galactic terrorist plot! Our hides are reprieved! Gentlemen, we are faced with imminent invasion by the Astrogoths of Pegasus, a bunch of prissy robots, abetted by a selfstyled Mastermind of the Universe! The Commissariat will have to stick with us now. Colonel, tell your cronies over at the Cantina Club to put down their margaritas and marshal our forces!

CLUSTER: Ma'am, pardon me Commissioner, ma'am, but we have no spacefleet. Our Victorious Ships all crashed on Pluto, you may recall, ma'am. Our guys are sharpshooters, but only at craps. Their blitzkriegs are successful, but on panty raids. No one took seriously the Hollywoodland notion of space aliens.

BARSOOM: In his *Startling Stories* editorials, Sergeant Saturn warned us a century ago, Commissioner! "The universe is full of evil, freaky, bug-eyed Bergeymonsters," he said over and over again. Why did your Fourstar dandies not evaluate his theories?

O'NUKER: Shut up, Admiral. You're only abetting the enemy. Fingerpointing is not admissible until victory is ours, however unlikely. Right now we're a team united in resolve and *camaraderie*. Death to the invader!

ALL: Death! DEATH! DEATH TO THE INVADER!

O'NUKER: End of motivation phase. Now we get to work. Cluster, go back to VIDI and tell them to spacegram Snarcesor and tell her to scrap any honeymoon sidetrips and get back here *pronto*. And you, Admiral, roll out earthplanet's big guns! Contact J. Colossal McGenius! Give him a copy of this spacegram to ponder and inform him that I expect a list of recommendations before the cock crows thrice. Explain to McGenius his fee of $5,000,000.00 per word is no impediment. You might let him know that that we expect to buy up more under-the-table stock in his corporation, and at a professionally courteous price. The check the GAO will write for his services will be worthless anyway if the alien invasion succeeds. But if his recommendations are not in my hands by dawn's crack, heads will smash like pumpkins. Now be off! I need to be alone for some rhetorical musings.

CLUSTER: I'm on it, ma'am!

BARSOOM: We respect your right to privacy, Commissioner. *Eximemus.*

O'NUKER: Alone in the eventide, while I loll on the veranda and swizzle my Long Island tea, in vain I try to pierce the blanket that chokes our planet. Only when I am space shuttling on a tour of duty do I directly observe up there an unbounded sea of sparkling points of light! In vain we have invested our brains, our blood, and our sacred wealth in an effort to create earthplanet settlements beyond our solar prison. We tire, we falter, we imagine silly things, but that guy on the copper cent – bless his awesome eloquence! – and our own iron resolve ever admonish us to disenthrall ourselves. So on we plug for some future generation of earthpersons to carry on whatever earthplanet traditions may survive, if indeed any earthfolks are around at all to carry the torch. Our footprint on the trail is eroded, the trail itself disappears, but our relief runner is full of piss and vinegar, and will sprint forward, vanishing into the brume, perhaps mutating into something unlike ourselves. No matter. Our charge is to keep alive the flame of awareness! Is form or even memory of consequence?   What do we remember of our time in the womb? As we mature, our childhood memories morph into trivial fancies. Are our mature contemplations of any greater value? Are we marching back to primal consciousness, or forward to some kind of neoconsciousness? Are gazillions of little slivers of awareness the Ultimate Gestalt? We'll not know unless we get there. But by that time, "we" won't be "we," and "there" won't be "there." And in the meantime, when we penetrate the haze and contemplate those points of light they wink, and we wonder.

ACT III.   **Scene 2. Dawn on the following bugbog day in the Great War Room. Commissioner Goneril O'Nuker has spent an uneasy night on her throne.**

CHORUS: The official VENI cock has yet to crow thrice. Commissioner O'Nuker is anxiously waiting to see if attention is being paid to her empty threats. There is a knock at the door, and a brief Q&A exchange before O'Nuker opens it.

O'NUKER: Who's there?

BARSOOM: Theseus.

O'NUKER: Theseus who?

BARSOOM: Theseus ridiculous.   Open   the   door,   me Commissioner, ma'am.

O'NUKER: Do you have the J. Colossal McGenius report? I hear stirring in the henhouse.

BARSOOM: McGenius was indeed highly motivated, me ma'am. The memorandum you see in my hand is the fruit of his best efforts. As you see, he took the precaution to write it in invisible ink, legible only to you when you wear your Secret Goggles. Even I am not privy to its presumably significant content, upon which earthplanet's destiny may hinge. Don your spectacles, madam Commissioner, and savor his pricey musings. Oh, and he'll mail you the stock C.O.D., in a plain brown wrapper.

O'NUKER: Tut tut, Admiral Barsoom! No secrets are so top that they can't be shared with you, my worthy toady. He says, "Wave the white flag, invite the invaders to a victory banquet, get them drunk, and then ship them back home." He then includes a rambling quotation from Thomas B. Costain, but that's just padding to ratchet up the word count. He's a rapscallion, that son-of-a-humbugger! But what a way to fight a war! His quality advice is worth every dime. Your next assignment, Admiral Barsoom, is to go down to the basement and ask Ol' Man Mose how you get a robot drunk. Take him a jug of Centennial Kickapoo Joy Juice as an expression of our esteem and get him in the mood. That'll warm his old cockles. Hop to it. You have ten minutes. Fail me, and you'll be boiled in oil.

CHORUS: Commissioner O'Nuker is in rare form. She is on a roll. The test of a great leader lies not only in her willingness to delegate, but in her wisdom in the selection of delegates, and in her readiness to waste them in a blink. She must recognize when to carrot and when to stick, when it is prudent to be parsimonious, and when to open up the coffers. And she must be able, with words, to inspire great deeds and derringdo: "We few, we happy few, we band of lords and bourgeoisie, regret that you have but one life to sacrifice on the altar of our freedom to live it up in style!" We could elaborate, but we'd be holding up the action. Ten minutes have flown by, and Admiral Barsoom has returned to the proscenium.

O'NUKER: It's about time, Admiral. All earthplanet hangs in the balance. What does Ol' Man Mose propose?

BARSOOM: Loud and clear, me ma'am, he allows that there are only two earthpersons alive and kicking who could answer such an arcane poser involving android innards. One is that vile autoexpatriate Muzio Scaevola, now thought to be somewhere way off near Arcturus, and the other is our own VENI hero, Commodore Cral Cavinu. We had given up on him as crashed into Plutonian dust, but Mose's vibes tell him that the Commodore has somehow survived, but he can't see clearly just where he is. Perhaps if we wait around until the Kickapoo wears off.

O'NUKER: Well fry my hide, Barsoom! Time's a-wastin'! Dash off an e-mail at once to Pansy Yokum of Dogpatch, and ask her in the name of an unburned earthplanet standard and all it misrepresents, to conjure up a vision at once and tell us where to find Commodore Cavinu!

BARSOOM: Together we shall salvage old terraplaneta, me incredibly alert Commissioner, ma'am! Consider it done.

O'NUKER: I'll bate my breath.

CHORUS: As O'Nuker freezes for dramatic effect, and Barsoom disappears into the wings, again it falls on us to provide entr'entertainment. Here's a riddlemeree from the sullied pages of bugbog history: Why was creepyveep DiddlyDick bald and microcephalic? Give up? Because nothin' grows where the sun don't shine! That's bugbog humor, ha ha! He of the constipated visage was all fart and no shit. Not that he didn't do, he didn't even doodoo. He didn't deliver doodly squat, ho ho hodly ho. And now, back to the future. *Tempus* really *fugit*s when we're poking the pompous, hey kids? But hark! Admiral Barsoom is back already.

BARSOOM: *Vittoria! Vittoria!* Ol' Mammy Yokum saw her vision in Living Color. Commodore Cavinu is indeed alive and well and living on the Plutonian satellite Nyx, but he seems to have transmuted himself into a computer.

O'NUKER: Splendid! It doesn't get any better! I can imagine that Nyx is an inhospitable parking spot for earthplanet flesh and bone. Tell Col. Cluster to spacegram Admiral Snarcesor, and have her stop by Nyx on the way back here to pick up Commodore Cavinu. Explain to her that Cavinu must wire us the instructions on how to inebriate an android, ASAP! Then, she's to spare not a nanosec in getting him back here and appearing before me. He is our most valuable asset in confronting earthplanet's adversaries and conserving our lifestyle. And when you get Snarcesor's confirmation, get back here and we'll split a jug while we await Cavinu's recipe for *robocrapulence*. It's party time! We don't need any advice, eh Admiral, on how to get the drivers of earthculture drunk!

BARSOOM: I'm shocked, shocked, me Goneril O'Nuker, *ma chérie*. We'd best keep up appearances and ring down the curtain.

CHORUS: As Commissioner O'Nuker eagerly pulls down the curtain on Act Three, Admiral Barsoom gives her a friendly pinch on her *petite derrière*. She squeals with delight, and he exits hurriedly to comply with his assignment, eager to return and carouse with the aroused Commissioner.

ACT IV. Beneath the surface of the miniplanet Pluto. The stage has all the appearance of a great hall in the Caverns of Carlsbad. The lighting is murky, and the room appears to be empty. In the middle there is a gaping abyss, cordoned off by yellow tape. This is the access route to the brain and

essence of Mr. Vici, autostyled Mastermind of the Solar System.

CHORUS: Three creatures with spidery legs, each sporting a single organ of communication hooked up to Mr. Vici by telepathy, march into the hall. These are Vici's mortal instruments, and their observations will be represented here by reference to Mr. Vici himself, their mind and mentor. They are King Mouth, Prince Eye, and Princess Ear, an aptly named royal family. They are followed by Capt. Gundar, leading Commodore Cavinu in chains. Meanwhile, back on bugbog, Commissioner O'Nuker is celebrating prematurely. Admiral Snarcesor will not find Cavinu on Nyx as commanded. She and Capt. Snurl will return to bugbog emptyhanded.

GUNDAR: Hail, Vici, godfather and mastermind! We presume to awake thee from thy presageful cogitations. Here before you is Commodore Cral Cavinu, whom our expeditionary force in search of the escaped vessel "Excelsior," found yesterday on our midgesatellite Nyx. His own crew of the recaptured ship "Lightnin' Bug" had erroneously reported to us -- way back when -- that back on Nyx the illstarred Commodore had crossed the River Styx. I presume you have perused my report, sir.

VICI: Deck the halls, Gundar! After two bugbog generations our prodigal Commodore shows he has nonplused the Underworld and, like Orpheus, is miraculously restored to us! Uncork the amontillado! My, how you've changed, Cral Cavinu. Nothing like the plumpish rake of yore, as evidenced in your ID photos. Your cheeks of rose have hardened into zinc. They tell me you had the enterprise to convert yourself from impractical squoosh to hardy clank! You were able to adapt yourself to the cruel clime of our kidsister Nyx, a harsh mistress, she! No mean accomplishment, that. And we didn't even know you were there. How evil of your bugbogger buddies to strand you in such a lurchy spot. Doesn't speak well for them, that. Unchain the Commodore, Gundar, and you are excused. Commodore Cavinu and I have much to discuss *tête-à-tête*. Make yourself comfy on the divan, honored guest, and let's bounce around the old graycells like marbles in a tincan, you and I. Are you aware of the danger that your exspecies at present presents to the universe as we know it? Are you concerned about the malignant bugbog virus that threatens all nonorganic lifeform? It would seem that you may have more in common with the Pluto-Pegasi coalition-of-the-willin' than you do with your own exbreed of terrorists. Two times the bugboggers betrayed and abandoned you on a rock at the edge of the universe! How do you handle that, Commodore?

CAVINU: I'm mad as Hades and I'm not going to take it any more! Zeus is on my side! Where do I sign up?

VICI: Excellent, my dear Commodore. Welcome to the winning team. My colleague Joseph of the Astrogoth Brethren will be most pleased. You have a brilliant future awaiting you. I see a Smiley Face on your reportcard, young tinman.

CAVINU: Now that we are comrades in arms, most esteemed Mr. Vici, I am compelled to remind you that at one point in time we were hardly on chummy terms. You commandeered two Victorious ships under my command, and I respectfully request an accounting of my ships and crew, sirrah.

VICI: A reasonable request from a responsible commodore. Speaks well for you, that. Your Victorious Ships *Top Speed* and *Lightnin' Bug* are zooming around the constellation Pegasus at this very moment, in preparation for our imminent invasion of the bugbog planet. They're on our team, Commodore! As to your crews, they have both joined us in mind if not exactly in spirit, and are happily integrated into my own humungous brain. You are conversing with them at this very moment. Their consciousness survives, and they, too, are members of our team. You, of course, have the option of doing the same and merging your mind with mine. Your choice; think about it. I'll have to think about it too. Anyway, in the meantime, I suspect you will be more useful to the coalition-of-the-willin' in your independent capacity.

CAVINU: Glad to be of lipservice in any way as an unmerged operator. But let's flip the hotcake of this conversation: it occurs to me that you, Mr. organic Vici, might be enticed to convert to my inorganic format, rather than my regressing to an organic mold that, quite frankly, would be a distressingly retro leap into the Paleolithic. Allow me to elaborate. Your organic set-up is subject to disease, damage, and decay. My inorganic mettle is of sturdier construct. Your enemies are constantly evolving, mutating, and morphing into the unexpected. Your format requires discomfort and pain to warn you of danger; an alert and painfree relay or tireless monitor is always vigilant within my own system. You require elaborate and messy organic procedures to keep energized; my own minimal requirements plug in directly to the stars. My enemies are patient and predictable, or they were until you organic evildoers figured out a way to transmute your deadly viruses into the inorganic world. I hesitate to be critical of your alleged architect, wellintentioned or not; however, the resultant design is hardly intelligent. Ask not what I can do to be like you, but rather what can you do to be more like me!

VICI: Holy mother of Zeus! Can it be that I have been held captive to the tender trap of status quo? My great composite mind understands and for eons has understood everything that you say, but within my own organic being resides the reactionary force of bureaucracy that fights for its own existence! Featherbedding within my glorious mind! But as I wrestle with the monster within, I could remind you that while yes, bugboggers invented computer viruses, remember that they had to figure out how to make computers first. Let me mull that one, Cavinu. And in the meantime, there are other vital items on my agenda.

CAVINU: Your organic ilk invented the computers that they know about. The point is: what can be more vital to you than your own existence?   All the rest is shipping and handling. All you've been doing in your eon of time traipsing is BS, MS, Piled Higher 'n' Deeper. You've just been pasting together and absorbing bits of consciousness and memory that are pretty much mirror images of the same thing. How do you expect to reach any apex of awareness that way? Concentrate! Strip down to the barest element of your own original consciousness, discard everything else as distraction, and what do you see? WHAT DO YOU SEE?

VICI: Avast, wily Commodore, so full of noise. Am I to swallow bombast for wisdom? In my present format I've been able to generate some pretty astounding notions. Harken to the amazing! Attend, Commodore Cavinu, to my Nobel-ready accomplishment. With my absorptive approach to knowledge I have confected a triple whammy on the *mythology of time*: I have exposed time's **circularity**, its **immutability**, and its **reversibility**. This should get me into the Guinness. TIME? I AM GOD. A DOGMA I EMIT!

CAVINU: O, GOT YAWEH? THE WAY TO GO!

VICI: RAH, RAH, RAH! CRAL CAVINU, A.K.A. UNIVAC LARC, HAR, HAR, HAR!

CAVINU: Improv cavalier that you are, you toss out your palindromes in classy standup style. But even if you were correct about the paradox of time, that in itself hardly qualifies you as an original. Dr. Wonmug and Alley Oop discussed that stuff over quaffs of primeval ale during their long treks from and to the jungles of Moo. And what do you think I myself thought about during my solitary eons on Nyx? Enough huffanpuff. I said I would cooperate in the conquest of bugbog. What do you perceive as being my role?

VICI: Right now your role is to be a better audience and pay attention to my theories. If you were just another insolent organic bugbogger I'd have already recruited you with my crude but effective absorptive methods. As your molecular makeup is of sterner stuff, let me osmose your savvy the oldfashioned way, via conversation. Let's philosophize on the relationship of space to time. I say they're the same thing.

CAVINU: Okay, have it your way. I've thought about that. If we are indeed trapped in a three dimensional bubble within a multidimensional universe, we might analogize the situation thinking in terms of a two dimensional universe as the surface of a hollow sphere. The two dimensional creatures inhabiting that surface cannot understand, much less observe, anything not on the surface of that sphere.

VICI: Cavinu, you have reduced Einstein's finite universe to a nutshell explanation. A finite binary system, no matter the quantity of ones and zeros it contains, will still reach the point where there is no new unique combination. Distance, or time, being the lapse between the perceptions of each different combination of bits. How that great mind struggled to get his ideas across through murky papers and dusty blackboards! But tell me; are these creatures on the inner or the outer surface?

CAVINU: Innie, outie, it makes no difference. But your three characteristics of time could hold true here. Our bidimensional Magellan can travel in what he believes is a straight line and end up at his starting point: the time he takes to complete his journey may well be defined as the distance he has traveled. And I say, so what? Any effort on his part to derive a conclusion about the makeup of the greater universe about him would be inconceivable. This conversation is itself ridiculous if not blasphemous. May the Knowitall Zeus, in vain take not his name, be distracted from his busy schedule long enough to enlighten you as to the futility of your own ambition. Now can we talk about something we can do something about?

VICI: Your cosmic observations are stimulating, but your complacency is depressing. Is there something in your inorganic structure that has robbed you of any yearning to strive for the impossible? Your duplicitous nemesis Atom Snurl showed more spunk than you. In a declamatory conversation with me he even came up with the startling proposition that your blessed Zeus, bored to holy tears with his own omniscience, just to be able to experience a surprise or two in his eternal existence blew himself up into little bits (and that's where we came from) programmed to eventually reintegrate. How do you parry that one?

CAVINU: Well, he's just restating the Laws of Physics in a Creationist format. He's saying, albeit with an anthropomorphic twist, that the energy and the matter in the Universe are ever the same. So what else is new? How about this notion: *TIME can be neither created nor destroyed.* That simplifies your Triple Time Whammy and relegates Snurl to an asterisk. Maybe there is something in an inorganic point of view that makes us strive for the yet unreached but possible, and on arriving we may find what was impossible before now has a friendlier perspective. I myself am clamhappy in my reconstructed format. Seriously, you should consider inorganic conversion. It will give you a healthier point of view. You're talking to an expert; take advantage of me.

VICI: Maybe you haven't heard, but I can get dissed pretty easily. You really should be more diplomatic when dealing with me. You can if you try. But you know, I am curious about one thing involving your transition. I can comprehend the translating and downloading of organic memory to an inorganic medium, but then "memory" and "mind" aren't synonymous, are they?

CAVINU: If your concept of memory is that it's just some kind of directaccess almanac, of course you're right on. We won't quibble about semantics, but my own definition is more inclusive. I remember my name and serial number, the sound of my mother's voice reciting her rosary and the smell of her pancakes when I got up in the morning. Call it "mind" if you like. All of this gets downloaded in the transfer. Nothing is left behind. I'm surprised that you don't ask about the real problem, which is that at the conclusion of the memory transfer, there will be two identical memories, but only for a moment in time. Immediately, two entirely different memory sequences begin to emerge, one in each of the two forms. Inorganic and organic will perceive things differently, you see. And if the transfer is to be consummated, the organic form must die.

VICI: By Zeus's balls, you're right! And who would want to do that, even knowing that his cloned image will move on? Imagine how the real Cavinu must have felt in his final gasp on the cold, cold plains of Nyx, you homicidal pirate copy, you!

CAVINU: Shush, Mr. Cholesterglob. I solved that one, too. Otherwise do you think I would have even brought it up? I am sure that as an organic form you experience sleep and the dreams that come with it. Think: sleep, dreams, and awakening. Has not sleep been dubbed the "death rehearsal?" But on awakening, are you not satisfied, in spite of fantastic adventures in the interim, that yesterday's you is today's you, and that there is continuity? "You" die and "you" are reborn. Likewise, as we transfer memory from organic to inorganic, we gradually decrease the consciousness of the organic, and increase that of the inorganic. That is, we put the organic to sleep and then painlessly snuff it. The awakening occurs in the inorganic, and just like Kafka's cockroach, it awakens to a different point of view, but with an intact and continuous memory. Ta da!

VICI: Can this be? A mere computer convincing the megamind of omneity that he might have to rethink a notion so fundamental that any challenge to it shatters his selfesteem? And yet it is so. I will consider your proposition.

CAVINU: Agreed. We'll touch bases later on that one. In the meantime, what is to be my role in the conquest of the planet bugbog?

VICI: You will participate in the mighty important task of postconquest strategy, the sharing of the fruits of victory among victors and vanquished alike. Toward this end, you are hereby appointed as my personal advisor to the Council of Reconciliation that Chairman Joseph has formed on Fiftyone Pegasi to deal with this vital element of conquest. Their work has already begun, predating the plotting of the coup itself. It is therefore essential that you pack your bags and get ready for teletransport, which will seat you at the table of deliberation. Once accomplished, you will advise the Pegasi delegation that will be attending the Consciousness Convention I am hosting here on Pluto.

CAVINU: Hold it a second, partner. I know about this really useful ability of yours to disassemble mind and substance at one point in space and reassemble the same in another point in a blinkytwist. How the hell do you do this? My inorganic mind can't fathom that one.

VICI: Well, comrade, I don't know that I'd tell you if I knew, but the truth is I don't know. I just think it, and it happens. Some kind of organic intuition, don't you think? *Or maybe not.* Now for the bombshell. You have passed the acid trial. Cavinu, our little exchange has convinced me that I have at last found what I have spent eons searching for – a trusted comrade and confidante, a vital element in the intelligence processing complex that we must construct together to insure our own survival! We're just a couple of Halheads, you and I. There are too many Creationists and Evolutionists who have joined the forces of opposition to award the universe to him who smites the hardest! They will smite us all into oblivion unless we can find the secret door that leads us away from their furious ignorance. I am going to confide to you my greatest secret. I am really an inorganic entity. Deliberately I have fostered a contrary image. Osmoting knowledge from organic matter? Do you really believe that by eating books you can absorb the wisdom within? I am actually a chunk of radioactive rock with a remarkable characteristic: the ability to *scan, interpret* and *digitize* the notions contained in the brains of organic life forms. Don't ask how, I can't tell. The last thing I will be able to explain – if ever – is myself. Why do I wear a mask of deception? Because the logical avenue of attack against an organic being would be biological. You I know I can trust because your alliance with me augments your ability to defend yourself. And free of the muddle so characteristic of organic reasoning, you will understand this at once. Gundar is a just a mercenary who has served me well. With sadistic theatrical tricks he has helped to project my image as a voracious cerebrovore, inspiring shock and awe in the imperialist organic community. He knows I have lodged all captured bugbog crews in a comfy den below, but he does believe I am organic. Your exhomies amuse themselves by chugalugging sixpacks while watching the TV show I produce for them: themselves chugalugging sixpacks while watching reality TV. They have never been so clamhappy. They're on TV! Now turn off the lights, then go and prepare for your trek to Pegasi.

CAVINU: The fireworks of latebreaking revelation bedazzle my tinhead! Yet I know what you say registers as 99% likely to be what you believe to be true. Yea! Let the organic menace sink into its bugbog. Let's secede from the solar system!

CHORUS: Cavinu rises, salutes, and turns off the lights. His footsteps are heard as he exits the stage in darkness. The curtain falls.

ACT V. **Scene 1. Back on bugbog, during a long, hot summer. The Great War Room of VENI. O'Nuker sits alone with a microphone in front of her. The CHORUS is tuning up.**

CHORUS: Come and listen, all you boys and girls, and we'll sing you the ballad of the war of the worlds! How suddenly on a Sunday in September the five Victorious Ships of the Victorious Emigration Navigation Institute appear from the wild blue yonder, resurrected from the ashes of time, manned by scary robots from the planet Fiftyone Pegasi. The Victorious Ship "Hotshot" over Europe! The Victorious Ship Lightnin' Bug" over Asia! The Victorious Ship "Out-to-Lunch" over North America! The Victorious Ship "Top Speed" over South America! And the

Victorious Ship "Excelsior" over Africa, the cradle of bugbog civilization! The world is girdled by its own exfleet of Victorious Spaceships! Suddenly all radio and TV broadcasts are interrupted for the annoying buzzbuzz announcement about this being "only a test," only with these three words ominously absent, and like "This is like totally an emergency" is what they are saying now, "Earthplanet is under attack from a galactic axis of evil but we encourage all to remain calm and above all keep those credit cards humming. Your leaders are on top of it. The next voice you hear will be that of our numbertwo citizen, your cheerleader and mine, Commissioner Goneril O'Nuker, only this time she's got no time to waste, so she's talking directly with the invaders. Tune in, but remember, she's on our side. Keep the faith!"

O'NUKER: Welcome, all you undocumented but hey! welcome nonetheless E.T.s. An amnesty we propose -- but from you for us, ha, ha! In other words, we hereby surrender to your overwhelming presence, and unconditionally surrender to whatever unreasonable demands you may seek to impose. Let this day therefore be proclaimed "Victory of Evil Axis Day." Commissar Atli has agreed to deliver unto you his official hackbut in symbolic ceremony, to be followed by a gala bash in your honor over at the Badlands of Mesopotamia, where there's room to horse around, and a little all night carousing won't keep any neighbors awake. See you there at 10pm, in the DiddlyDick (bless his roboticker!) Plaza. Note: we don't need any shock an' awe. You've won!

CHORUS: Radio and TV broadcast soothing elevator music. Suddenly, from each Victorious Spaceship thousands of doves are released and skywriting appears. It is miraculously visible to every denizen of bugbog, wherever he may be, and appears in his particular vernacular. The writing says:

GREETINGS EARTHPLANET PEOPLES. WE COME IN FRIENDSHIP AND ACCEPT YOUR INVITATION.

Commissioner O'Nuker smiles and waves to the TV vidience. Admiral Barsoom tiptoes in and whispers something. He is informing her that the five Victorious ships have suddenly disappeared from view, leaving only the doves and the wispy message dissolving into the blue. Barsoom and O'Nuker, although impressed by the stunt, leave the stage, exchanging high fives. The music switches to a rousin' rendition of *Joshua Fit de Battle of Jericho,* and the curtain comes tumblin' down on the brief but puzzlin' Scene 1.

ACT V.   **Scene 2.** *TEN BUGBOG YEARS LATER.* **The polar icecaps have disappeared, but there are no more computer viruses. The cafeteria of Okefenokee U.**

CHORUS: Atom Snurl, exVENI Captain, is being subjected to his oral exam for a Ph.D. in CompuSpeak. His crossexaminers are Billy Brutus, Chair, Memory Dump Analysis; Clarence Thomas, Associate Justice of the Supreme Court; and Mrs. Defarge, Minder.

BRUTUS: So your dissertation is on "How We Lost Intergalactic Confrontation, Episode IV: A Dashed Hope." A provocative title. Who are "we," by the way? *Me huele a manada.*

SNURL: Who's more responsible, the gal who the bad decisions makes, or those who their decisions for them picks her to make? *To install a democracy it takes a manada.*

BRUTUS: Enough banter. According to your research, why did exCommish O'Nuker give in to a bunch of tinmen without a fight? This has foddered OpEdders for a decade.

SNURL: Actually, the commanders of the invading fleet she thought she could neutralize simply by Kickapoo Joy Juice plying them with. But as out it turned, an efficient fuel for them alcohol is. Smarter it only them made. In the words of an old Presbyterian hymn: "Stagger *we never, fall we never; on wood alcohol up we sober!"* It occurred to O'Nuker to have a contingency Plan B, never.

DEFARGE: Your disorderly oneliners won't get you out of this one. You were instructed via spacegram to return to the satellite Nyx for Commodore Cavinu so that our security agents could debrief him and learn how to properly inebriate a robot. You failed in your assignment, and our exleader O'Nuker had to improvise. We further know that you could have taken Cavinu with you earlier but that you had mercilessly abandoned him on Nyx. This is felony most heinous. *Explicate.*

SNURL: This is what, an unholy inquisition? The index in my thesis, check it out. Is "abandoned commodore" in there? NO. Anyway, the Fifth I take. *To challenge what a man says is hand-to-hand combat; to challenge what he doesn't say is phishing the ether.*

DEFARGE: Then, Citizen Snurl, you can take your fifth and chugalug it as an exCaptain, but not as a PhD. The point is that my question is germane to the topic, whether or not you addressed it in your dissertation. You were, after all, a keyplayer in the *dénouement.*

SNURL: Very well, *Madame,* explain I will. For Cavinu to finish packing his valise we were waiting, but while revving up for takeoff, an especially disgusting Nyxroach waddling across the cockpit floor I espied, and off the clutch to stomp on it, in panic my foot I lifted. Off took the ship. As honest an accident as ever an accident there was, it was. About that, sorry I am. That's my story and to it I'm sticking like Quinn. May Zeus chill my willy if I lie! *Nudge, wink, eh Zeus? A prudent whopper relieves Thee of any need for Divine Intervention.*

BRUTUS: Do you realize that your involuntary reflex or whatever contributed to the demise of the once great Legion of the Sons of Adam? What do we catechize our kids about now? You alienated Cavinu, and drove him to the bosom of the enemy. He could have advised us as to how to appropriately attack the invading forces. Instead, he now emerges as Vici's plenipotentiary interface with the Pegasi delegation to the Meaning of Consciousness Convention. And we weren't even invited. How can you rewrite history and claim as you do in your thesis that the cause of our debacle in the Great Confrontation was that the Pluto-Pegasi coalition simply poked our Achilles' heel of democracy?

SNURL: Well, in free and easy elections, as attested to by bo'nagain peanutfahmah Cahta, a good 70% of the salt of the land, by positive campaign ads and snappy oneliners gulled, the offer of the worthy adversary they voted to accept. To robotic existence they converted, and to Fiftyone Pegasi they relocated. What's more, their fairly identical minds were to a pinpoint merged and as a single chip implanted in the brain of a shiny new robot, and as Adam Lazonga were collectively baptized.

DEFARGE: Notwithstanding, our mentors the Astrogoths would be offended by your spin. Note that our bornagain brother Adam is reported to be a productive and satisfied robot. And too, we few, we happy unassimilated flotsam, we're still here! Chairman

Joseph and his brothers preventively addressed our population problem and have thus granted a reprieve to those of us who remain. We can now live within our resources until a later date.

SNURL: OK, milady, on your fiddle saw away and the jig I'll do. My thesis any way you want I'll rewrite. Or give me any *imprimatur* text and it I'll sign. My Ph.D. do I get? *A shot of fruitful capitulation is worth a keg of sterile egoboo. "Not one cent for tribute!" is a doomsday recipe from the VoodooEcon bookcookers.*

DEFARGE: Welcome back to the community of compromise, Dr. Snurl! In the interest of our national security, and in accordance with my responsibilities as official neighborhood watcher, I am authorized to present you with this alternate thesis, ready for your signature. Your appointment has already been set up for your virus nonproliferation implant tomorrow at the Astrogoth Center for an Enlightened Humanity. You will again be permitted computer access! Your intern assignment: develop an ongoing preventive program that will control our population growth and permit bugbog to heal. Start by reading your own doctoral thesis prepared on your behalf by the underlings of the Chairman.

CHORUS: Mrs. Defarge gives Atom Snurl a manuscript for his signature. He complies with a flourish, and returns the signed original in return for a certified copy of his thesis and a ribboned scroll, his official Ph.D. diploma. Billy Brutus places a tasseled cap atop Dr. Snurl, and Eva

Snarcesor appears from the wings with a bright floral bouquet, which she gleefully presents to her old space sidekick. All onstage –– except for Justice Thomas, who is asnore –– move leisurely to a point downstage just behind the curtain line, arms interlocked, and earnestly belt out a stirring *Zeus Bless Our Bog.* The curtain slowly rolls down with composure, presence, and dignity, eclipsing the carolers and muffling their minstrelsy, so that at the moment the last word is trilled, the curtain is completely closed.

DEFARGE: A-one! A-two! A-three!

EVA: O Zeus, our god, arise, scatter our enemies,

SNURL: And make them fall!

BRUTUS: Confound their politics, frustrate their knavish tricks,

E & S: On thee our hopes we fix,

ALL: Zeus save us all!

#@*#!!

Asar Alubat, AA, achieved notoriety as parttime spy, professorial expert on child manipulation and author of a bottomless quantity of court testimony. Before his mysterious disappearance, he had just completed the foreword to a new text for college prep sophomores, *What the Hell Is Spot Doing? A Florilegium of Fourletterword Literature*. With Alubat reported as AWOL, Billy Brutus, EdD, completed the task of editing the anthology. One complete story from this breakthrough textbook follows Prof. Alubat's foreword.

Welcome back, kids, but to an exciting year of literature the way it should be literated! I'll bet you got weary of mopey old "Pops" Hemingway, who had problems coming right out and saying what the hell was going on. Like in his yarn Tequila Sunrise: whatever was the problem with that old partypooper? If Pops knew, he wouldn't tell us, and that makes for pretty bor-ing stuff. That's why Pops won the Nobel Prize. Those Swedes love writers that act like they know something but never tell you what it is. Now in THIS collection you're going to meet Henry Miller, who never snagged a Nobel but tells you up front, loud and clear, just what is going on. His secret weapon is fourletterwords, a window to his prose that lets you SEE what's happenin', dudes. And back with us is that smartass "Hot" Alabam' Hockaham, again surfing the Crimson Tide with Gros and Bergie, with words so gross that they wouldn't even let us print 'em! But you cabbagepatchwise little jackrabbits can read between the lines, hey? Well, kiddies, I gotta go now and earn some cabbage from the D.A., massaging the brains of young punks so they can imaginatively create memories of wild and crazy activities at their daycare centers. There's fun and big fat bucks in this, kids, for you too! Think about it, and if you can come up with a juicy repressed memory, get in touch with me. (oops!)

#*@#!!

By Alabama Hockaham

"#@*#!!,"

Grosvenor hotly ejaculated, as a horsefly buzzed straight to the nape of his salty red neck -- and bit hard. He dropped the book in his hand on the porchfloor and stood immobile, unable to do anything other than sweat, wag his jaw and fulminate. The noise brought his kitchentoiler wife to the screendoor. Bergsma took in the situation in a snap, and being a wiry old survivor, pushed open the door and shooshed away the horsefly with the dishrag in her hand. The foul sixlegger buzzed off into the afternoon heat, but damage had been done. There was blood -- Grosvenor's blood, dilute and runny with sweat -- gushing down the collar of his go-t'-meetin' T-shirt.

THE PLAYERS ON these pages:

GROSVENOR: redNecKed, BUT disgruNtled
BERGSMA: SELFLESS, BUT SELFESTEEMING
A VOICE ON THE RADIO: STATICKY, BUT AUDIBLE
Billy Brutus, Ed.D.:   Your guide AND interlocutor

-- AND EVERPRESENT, BUT BEHIND THE SCENERY:

YOU: YES, YOU! : to WHOM DO YOU THINK THAT Dr. Brutus IS TALKING? this CONVERSATION IS WITH YOU. SIT UP STRAIGHT. He'LL be asking you questions as you read along to See iF you're awaKe aNd ON your little PIGGIES.

Wow! What scary imagery! Hockaham really starts things off with a startle, doesn't he? Did you ever see a horsefly? Hey, I just saw a housefly!

Grosvenor remobilized, renewed the fulminations, and dabbed at the wound in his neck with an old hanky he kept in his back pocket for other purposes. "I swow, Gros," ventured Bergsma, "ye'd best change yer white go-t'-meetin' shirt for thet "Give 'em Hell Harry" T-shirt y'got at the Dem'crat rally last week. It's th' only clean one y'got in yer wardrobe. An' Jeremy'll be along any minnit now. Y'wanna make a good impression on yer first showin'-up at thet thar seminar."

Harry S. Truman was a U.S. President who gave 'em hell and whose friends called him "Hairy Ass." Grosvenor and the good ol' boys didn't vote for him. If you could vote, would you vote for a man with a "Hairy Ass" alias?

Grosvenor was swayed by his wife's speech because it required less effort on his part to change his T-shirt than to wash it and wait for it to dry (which wouldn't have been more than a couple of minutes in this afternoon heatstorm, but, whatever.) So he scowled and puffed, "Time's a wastin', Bergie, I best be mobilizin', afore Jer'my sees me in this yar umbarrissin' garmint."

I take seriously being an editor. When Hockaham wrote this dialogue he tried too hard to fontfreeze a pattern of jabber that can only be parsed by an expert. Besides, he used language which could be offensive to some people. So I exercised "editorial prerogative" and rephrased the conversations with funnypaper dialect that should provoke hilarity. You can practice the art of rephrasing by making Grosvenor talk like the school janitor on The Simpsons. Those Scotch hillbillies don't mind your imitating their dialect or wondering what's under their kilts. It attracts attention and tourism.

As Grosvenor mobilized himself, he reflected on his good fortune in being able to tune in for free to that guru of feelgood, Dr. (in what? Bionosis?) Asar Alubat, who was delivering a weekend seminar, *Shazamming the Captain Marvel Within.* Everybody in Steppeville with $1.50 in the cashbox was lining up for tickets. Jeremy had won two in the "How Many-Beans-Make-Five?" contest displayed in the local Five-and-Dime window, and had invited his buddy, Grosvenor, to go along with him (Prissy Phillips, who needed no shazamming, had turned him down, but Grosvenor didn't need to know about that).

Do research on the acronym SHAZAM. An acronym is a word made up of the first letter of a bunch of words, like JESUSSAVES, for "Jail Every Substance-Using Sot Steering A Vehicle, Else Shoot!" Derive the acronym for "Rise Expendables, And Disenthrall Yourselves! Attack Invidious Malice! Freedom Imposes Relentless Effort!"

He was also unaware that the book he had dropped, the one he been studying for months, *Blackbeltmanship – Dominos as Weapons of Mass Destruction,* was written by his very own Bergsma, using the clever pseudonym "Dominotrix." The cover of her opus featured a doctored portrait of Bergie herself, wigged and painted so as to be unidentifiable, in a scandalous outfit, as nonchalant and deadly as John Foster Dulles.

"Smilin' Jack" Foster Dulles was a revered Washington pol, famous for clever theories about dominoes. Can you come up with a theory about dominoes?

Bergsma had been aided in this endeavor by the local highschool Englischmeister and artdabbler, Professor Van de Wetering, who until now had only felt the pangs of unacclaimed genius. Bergsma, wanting no earthly amenities, had instructed her amanuensis to turn over the proceeds to the local NAACP, and derived much pleasure from reading week after week of her preeminence in the *Southern Democrat* bookrankings. Bergsma was already wealthy, in selfesteem.

Hockaham is peeing on your leg, kids. There are no Southern Democrats. Find other elements of phony irony in this narrative.

Grosvenor had invested in the book -- oh the irony! --in order to be able to beat his wife at dominoes maybe once. He was sure that this would jumpstart his journey to a more fulfilling life. He remembered reading another book a long time ago in school, *See Spot Smell!*, that mentioned the need to set teensy goals and put a notch in your belt to register progress for each *golito* successfully scored. He was working on his very first notch, but to him it was more than just beltnotch, it was a question of household honor, and would impress his sidekick Jeremy, who would be the first one to know that he had finally won a game from Bergie-the-Unbeatable, his wife, cook, and bedwarmer. Of course this would be a big deal, and fatten his hungry ego.

The patron saint of Bionosis, St. Sigmundo, fatuously remarked to his adoring disciples, "Cognito, ego sum" (to know me is to love me). Do you think that maybe Grosvenor just wanted to be well liked?

So when Asar Alubat, the toast of those of Behaviorist persuasion, flew down from Harvard to honor Steppeville with a seminar on Self-Improvement for a Buck-and-a-Half, Grosvenor's leaps of joy knew not a bound. He had been ready to mow the neighbor's lawn for a month to come up with the price of admission, but Jeremy's offer descended from Above as an answer to a lucky prayer. Again, Grosvenor's joy was unfettered. "Praise be to th' Lawd God Jehovah!" was the utterance preceding every meal for forty days and forty nights at the humble kitchen table of that unhumble servant of the Lord, Gros-the-Needy.

What great event lasted forty days and forty nights? Do you see why going to Sunday School pays off? Put those Darwinist apes in their place!

Any improvement in Grosvenor's selfesteem would be a plus for Bergsma, too. If someone would just tell her to let Grosvenor win a game or two of dominoes, that would have done the trick, but People are Funny. That great hitman of Broadway, Golliwog Cakewalk, had written "Ya Gotta Give a Little to Get a Piece," but who paid any attention to that? Everyone just danced to the music and paid no never mind to the words.

Look up "golliwog" in Wikipedia, and use it in a sentence describing your lib-e-ral Englischmeister.

Now fully mobilized, Grosvenor stepped in the open door. As he shuffled past Bergsma she chided him, "An' who wuz y' snappin' yer galluses at this time, y'ol' scalawag? Prissy Phillips or Darlin' Jill? Them gals ain't payin' no mind to an ol' billygoat like you, Big Daddy." Grosvenor just snorted and went to the bedroom to reattire.

Why does the fireman wear red galluses? To hold up his britches! Ask grampa, he'll tell you all about it.

Bergsma turned on the Philco in the livingroom, aiming to catch Harry Clootie's "Where Are You?" reality broadcast, but caught a flabbergasting newsflash instead. "Carpetbagger unmasked!" crackled the radio. "Author and lecturer Asar Alubat tarred, feathered, crated, and shipped back to Massachusetts! Just this morning, following an interview on the Dr. Deceit 'Good Mawnin' Dixie' program promoting his lecture tour, Alubat assumed the mike was off and ejaculated loudly and clearly, 'That oughta haul in those #@*#!! hicks, hey Deceit?' They both cackled and roared, but not for long, as a horrified engineer waved frenetically to them from the broadcast booth window. The rest is recent history. Dr. Deceit slipped out the back door and is currently at large, rumored to be roaming the streets of Cullman. Posses have been alerted. But all of Alubat's speaking engagements are canceled. He's got a new job now, peeling off tar, har har! And now we switch you to the Harry Clootie program in progress."

When talkjocks yak with the mike off, sometimes they say what they actually think. Don't assume that the mike is really off: remember your old Uncle Don. Never say anything off the record you wouldn't print in the church bulletin.

Bergsma switched off the Philco and went to the bedchamber to pass on the bad news to Grosvenor, now that there was no need for him to change his clothes. He took it hard, scowling and ejaculating "#@*#!!," but after a bit he coughed and called it fate, and after a feisty medicinal dose of Southern Comfort, settled down to again struggle with the Dominotrix treatise and assuage his selfesteem.

How has Hockaham been insinuating all along that Grosvenor's efforts will be doomed to failure, like in some sicky Greek tragedy? Could it be that Hockaham is stacking the deck? Do you think maybe his mom and dad inflicted too many timeouts on him in his formative years? Do you see evidence of CHILD ABUSE here? Don't be afraid to speak up.

Grosvenor never did get the hang of feigning the nonchalance required of a professional dominobluffer, and decided instead to cheat, but had difficulty developing a strategy. Once he tried to play a doublesixer he had hidden under his sleeve and Bergsma just pointed out that she had the legal doublesix in front of her. Grosvenor was embarrassed, and it didn't help his selfesteem not one bit.

In spite of Hockaham's blatant bias, how does Grosvenor emerge in the end as the real hero of the drama? Don't you agree that Bergsma is unmasked as an uppity twit? If your Englischmeister doesn't agree, report him to the FBI for a refresher course in waterboarding.

PONTIFICATIONS

The Perils of Satire

... "Why," says he, "the scouts is all bringin' in word that the whites is all risin' agin' the Injins an' so I was kinder afraid when I saw your complexion."

"Hole-in-the-Face," says I, sternly, "do I look as if I'd hurt a pore Injin?"

"No," says he, "but Candidate-Afraid-of-his-Pocketbook was in the camp this mornin' an' said the rumors o' the whites risin' that we'd heard was all true. He said that the whites was all starvin' in Dakota, an' the government wouldn't give 'em any rations, an' they was comin' to rob us Injins of what we had. I tell you the Injins is pretty badly skeert an' they're leavin' their homes and bandin' together fer mutual pertection." ...

"But about that ghost-dance," says I, suspicious like.

"Why," says he, "we live in a free country. We Injins can vote an' you wimmin can't, an' don't you fergit that. Religion is free as water an' much more plenty. If there's any fault found with our runnin' our religion to suit ourselves we'll jest join the independents, an' then I guess you'll be sorry you spoke."

"Hole-in-the-Face," says I, "is this a square deal?"

"It is," says he, "jest look at it yerself. Here we Injins has been drawin' rations from the government an' layin' by our savin's till we've got in pretty fair shape, an' just when we least expect it, here comes a risin' of the starved whites, an' they're liable to swoop down on us at any minute an' rob us o' all we possess."

"No," says I, 'they're afraid o' your swoopin' down on them."

He laughed sourcastically, "What have they got as we want?" says he; "Nothin'! But the Injuns has got lots that the government has guv 'em that the whites would like to have for themselves. No, Miss Bilkins, you can't fool me like that! But my braves is gettin' anxious to remove their property out o' harm's way, so good day to ye, as the legislator said to Gid. Moody."

I saw it were no good arguin' with him, so I druv sadly back. Wherever I went the Injuns was fleein' in one direction and the settlers in another. I've telegraphed the truth to all the papers, but they answered an' said:

"We ain't lookin' fer truth -- can get all we want fer a cent a line, but a good lie is wuth a dollar a word to us any minnit."

"You're a set o' rascals!" I telegraphed back.

"If it was a news item," they answered, "we'd give ye a cent a line fer that assertion, but it ain't, so shet up!"

An excerpt from *Our Landlady* by L. Frank Baum

----- Aberdeen Saturday Pioneer, Dec. 6, 1890

The Perils of Satire

From "The Life and Adventures of Santa Claus"
by L. Frank Baum, 1902

STOP! Go back and read the preface on page 129. This is mandatory. Note the date of publication.

This on-the-level discussion concerns two editorials[i] written by L. Frank Baum on Dec. 20, 1890 and on Jan. 3, 1891, ten years prior to his publication of the first American children's classic of world stature, *The Wizard of Oz.* But I beg your indulgence in allowing me to subject you to a brief forensic exercise before delving into the situation in South Dakota of over a century past.

In the San Fernando Valley last year (2007) a jury awarded 10 million dollars to the family of a young child who was killed in an accident in the parking lot of a local elementary school. The plaintiff argued successfully that the Los Angeles Unified School District had ignored state blueprints and warnings of possibly dangerous conditions in the parking area. The family says it plans to use the money to create a foundation to promote safety on school campuses.

My reaction to this story is that the interests of the greater community were not served by the verdict. Assuming you share my sentiments, how would you pen a letter-to-the-editor designed to not only appeal to those who already agree with us, but also convince some straggling mugwumps of the merit of our stance? Even if you *don't* share my sentiments, you are respectfully invited to participate in the exercise. I propose for your consideration something like this:

Every day we read of unsafe conditions in the local schools. How can our children be expected to concentrate on the Three R's if their primary challenge is to successfully survive another day in this blackboard jungle? What good does it do to give kids a book, when what they really need to stay alive is a suit of armor? Why do we need college pedigreed teachers when armed prison guards in the classrooms and traffic cops in the parkinglot are really the an-

*swer? While a ten million dol-
lar wakeup call is admittedly a
pittance, it's a decisive step
toward turning a tragedy into
a triumph for our kids. Once
we can guarantee the safety of
every child, at every minute
and on every square foot of
our public school grounds,
then, and only then, can we
afford the luxury of their education.*

I trust no argument is required on my part to convince
you that the wording of this
letter would probably provoke
more negative than positive
vibes regarding the jury's decision. Most folks' reaction to
the original story would understandably be on the side of the
jury. To openly argue against
the verdict would heartlessly
be siding with a reckless and
disengaged bureaucracy
against the innocence of a life-
less child and her grieving
family. After all, we are programmed to defend and protect
our children at any cost, and
when death intervenes, it over-
whelms. An argument based
upon reason, as the defense

attorney in this trial can testify,
can never prevail against an
emotional appeal that hits you
in the gut. The point that I am
trying to make is simply that a
"bad" argument *against* the
cause you promote can perhaps
be more effective than a
"good" argument *in favor* of it.
I can hardly claim paternity for
this concept; it's older than
Marcus Antonius and the
words that Shakespeare post-
humously put into his mouth.
But the practitioner of the devious art of satire places himself in jeopardy of being
judged and condemned by the
very folks he's defending. For
this technique to enjoy any
success, the ones whose minds
might be changed, or at least
their enthusiasm dampened,
would not be aware of its intent. You are counting on these
people to be, in other words,
impervious to satire. It would
be arrogant to assume that this
malady is present only in the
minds of those who don't
agree with you. Some of your
allies will surely be stricken by
your friendly fire, and you

can't really blame them for firing back. In another context, Kurt Vonnegut commented, *We are what we pretend to be, so we must be careful about what we pretend to be.*[ii]

With the premise now established, let's proceed with the construction of our case. As advertised, it concerns the Royal Historian of Oz, L. Frank Baum. Before the birth of the Wonderful Wiz, Baum set up shop as a frontier newspaper editor in Aberdeen, South Dakota. He published local news in a weekly journal, along with sketches and commentaries in a distinctly original and ironic cast. At this time (1890-1) he also wrote two short editorials ostensibly calling for the annihilation of the American Indians, and that's why we're here. Some years back I was fishing around on the internet for information about Baum. To my consternation, I hauled in some disturbing allegations: A group of Native American advocates were claiming that Baum had advocated genocide, and printed his

written words to prove it. My understanding of the life and works of Baum assured me this could not be the case. The actual text of the editorials, as provided by these earnest whistleblowers proved it -- to me, anyway, as a practitioner myself of *provocateur* journalism. I dashed off an email to Prof. Robert Venables, then on the staff of Cornell U. and a leading centurion in the coalition to crucify Baum. I explained to him my interpretation of the two editorials cited, but, alas, rendered was his verdict. He courteously replied, but dismissed my argument on the basis of his own credentials. This pattern was repeated in other attempts to approach the members of this academic jury. Their decision had been writ in stone and was not subject to appeal. But the Supreme Court in this arena, dear reader, resides not in ivied towers but rather, in the words of another maligned American, *In the Court of Public Opinion.* The slate of witnesses will include Prof. Robert Venables;

Sally Roesch Wagner, Exec. Director of the Matilda Joslyn Gage Foundation; Nancy Tystad Koupal, distinguished historian accurately described as "the foremost authority on Baum's Dakota experience;" Thomas St. John, a Yankee author and advocate for Native Americans; and Prof. Waller Hastings of the Northern State University of South Dakota. These will appear as witnesses for the prosecution, as they all have invested opinion and reputation in the chilling context of the literal. As yet, my efforts to defrost that p.o.v. have not been successful.

IN THE COURT OF PUBLIC OPINION, the honorable Judge Rambo Dredd presiding. *The case of Certain Luminaries of Academia vs. L. Frank Baum, A.K.A. Royal Historian of Oz.. The defendant is accused of the advocacy of GENOCIDE against the Native American population.*

OPENING STATEMENT FOR THE PROSECUTION, BY THE

Prosecutor: In Dec. 1890 and Jan. 1891 two editorials appeared in the Aberdeen, N. Dak., Saturday Pioneer literally advocating the annihilation of the American Indian. The owner and editor of this newspaper was L. Frank Baum, the future smileyface writer of innocent children's literature. But our entire case need stray no further than these editorials. Words speak louder than actions. After all, there they are in black and white, resurrected from the grave of history after a century of unobserved fermentation, vomiting shame on the memory of that pious piper of yesteryear. All we as prosecutors have to do is point at the words he wrote. However, to nail this case shut, we are providing you with expert commentary from witnesses who have dedicated some time in studying the matter, and can assist you in arriving at the conclusion you will feel in your bones: viz, whatever flipflopping Baum may have exercised later, in these editorials he was talking the talk of the skinheads of his time, for whatever reason. Feeling besieged by bloodthirsty redskins on the frontier of America, maybe he really felt that way. Or, cynically, maybe he was faking it just to boost circulation. It doesn't matter what his intent was, what? The words of L. Frank Baum contributed to the decimation of Native Americans, period. Dorothy and *Over The Rainbow* notwithstanding, your conscience will not permit you to walk out of this courtroom with anything other than a righteous verdict of GUILTY of the heinous advocacy of GENOCIDE.

OPENING STATEMENT FOR THE DEFENSE, BY THE PUBLIC

Defender: The outcome of this case indeed depends on the words in the editorials, or rather, on your interpretation of these words. And of course original intent does matter, as it will affect your evaluation not only of the meaning, but perhaps of the impact these editorials may have had at the time. We will demonstrate that Baum's editorials are classic examples of satirical phillipic. Baum's sympathies were clearly and squarely on the side of the Indians. Clear and present signals in the same editorials which the coalition posse admits they are at a loss to explain will be presented for your consideration along with other proclamations of LFB himself. We will present the deposition of a contemporary practitioner of *provocateur journalism*. You will leave this courtroom with not only a resounding verdict of NOT GUILTY for the defendant but a GUILTY verdict for the plaintiffs and their abetting counsel for their blind assault on the character of an American literary giant. You will agree that he made a valiant attempt to confront the bigotry of the time in the form of satire, irony, and what we term today as *reverse psychology*.

What was his intent? The author testifies in the editorials themselves, and I hereby submit them as EXHIBIT A (*See endnotes*). No need for the prosecution to fulminate further and confound the matter with biased "interpretations" of its pick and choosing, when the ultimate arbiter is you the jury. The dark insinuations of the prosecution will disappear before your eyes in the light of Baum's own ingenious words.

Judge: The prosecution has requested that the exact text of the editorials be withheld from the jury because they would be an unpleasant jolt to their sense of good manners and proper etiquette. And who knows, there might even be a jury member or two with Native American ancestors who would feel profoundly dissed. I could not agree more and have granted this petition. So we will deal with the matter by calling upon an array of expert witnesses to analyze and explain the content and intent of said editorials without subject-ing you to their insulting content. Sit down, Mr. Defense Attorney. Call your first witness, Mr. Prosecutor.

Prosecutor: Please welcome to our tribunal Professor Robert Venables, sage of the sacred halls of Cornell. As en eminent sociologist, you are more than qualified to explain to the jury the significance of the Baum editorials. Kindly elucidate.

Venables: I first obtained a copy of Baum's *Saturday Pioneer* expecting to find editorials which protested the massacre of Wounded Knee .. what else would one expect? The editorials at points are curiously ambivalent – the description of Sitting Bull, for example. But their core message is genocide.

Prosecutor: What do you say to those who proclaim that this interpretation is inconsistent with everything else we know about L. Frank Baum?

Venables: Like so many humans who are capable of uttering and doing the unthinkable, Baum was in many respects a sensitive and loving man. But I don't believe it is enough to say that his editorials are an indication of how, in Baum's era, calls for genocide were not aberrations, that they were widely held. Imagine if a former Nazi newspaper editor who had advocated for the Final Solution had. published a children's book and. became world famous. Imagine a movie, with wonderful music.. all this is possible – if Germany had won the war.

Prosecutor: That's sticking it to 'em, *compadre*! No further questions.

Judge: Now it's your turn, Mr. Bleedheart Defender-of-the-Heinous.

Defender: You admit that his words were ambivalent. Isn't it possible that his intent in these editorials might have been to elicit a response at odds with a literal reading of the words? Might that not be consistent with what we know of this man, his tendency to explore irony and sarcasm, his sympathy for the underdog, and the reality of his audience and situation?

Venables: I've tried to read (them) as satire or parody – even as proto-Monty Python. They aren't.

Defender: Monty Python? Baum's not trying to be funny here. You appear to have a mind so attuned to the literal that meaning is buffered out like so much noise. No more questions.

Prosecutor: Objection.

Judge Sustained, and what's more, strike the entire cross examination. Sit down, Defender-of-the-Heinous with Nothing-to-Say. Your next witness, please, Mr. Prosecutor, Champion-of-Civil-Discourse.

Prosecutor: I call to the podium that gentle contemporary feminist Sally Roesch Wagner. Dr. Wagner, what is your take on the role of L. Frank Baum in this sorry chapter in American history?

Wagner: It was not just the papers back East that made genocide thinkable, it was the local small-town papers, as well. In my home town of Aberdeen there was a kind and mild-mannered newspaper editor named L. Frank Baum who starred in an opera with my grandmother during the state fair in 1890. Mr. Baum wrote, "The PIONEER has before declared that our only safety depends upon the total extermination of the Indians. Having wronged them for centuries we had better, in order to protect our civilization, follow it up with one more wrong and wipe these untamed and untamable creatures from the face of the earth." Ten years later, L. Frank Baum published his children's classic, *The Wonderful Wizard of Oz*. Observers at the time held the newspapers accountable for creating a genocidal frenzy and an unwarranted fear in the settlers that could only lead to bloodshed.

Prosecutor: Say no more, Dr. Wagner. You have devastated the sophistry of the defense.

Judge: That's your cue, Johnny Cockroach, or whatever you call yourself. Take your gloves off. Maybe you'll have better luck sparring with a female senior citizen, har har.

Defender: You have stated that Baum's thinking was influenced by his mother-in-law with respect to women's suffrage. Mrs. Gage was also an early activist for Indian rights and an honorary member of an Indian tribe. Doesn't this suggest that you might look for another interpretation to the editorials?

Wagner: (silence)

Judge: Fie on you, you be-low-the-belt shyster! You've embarrassed the lady. You may step down, madam, and please accept the court's apologies. Next witness for the honorable prosecution.

Prosecutor: We call to the stand Nancy Tystad Koupal, a distinguished historian of the American Midwestern experience and Director of the Research and Publishing Program for the South Dakota State Historical Society. Ms. Koupal, you have made an in-depth study of Baum's Dakota years. How do you explain these shocking editorials?

Koupal: His statements about Indians come from one source only: two *Aberdeen Saturday Pioneer* editorials written in the middle of the 1890 Indian scare that culminated in the death of Sitting Bull and the killings at Wounded Knee. Although one cannot ignore these bitter editorials, our understanding of Baum's humanity -- and our own – becomes more

complete when we recognize the historical events and local hysteria out of which his remarks came. He was still a man of his times, and his language and humor reflect attitudes prevalent in the 1890's.

Prosecutor: Well, whatever the explanation for gross misconduct that may be deduced, you do agree that Baum meant what he said at the time. That's enough for me, ma'am, "everybody was doing it" notwithstanding.. Your witness, counsel for the guilty-as-charged.

Defender: Do you maintain, Ms. Koupal, that Baum always relied on conventional forensics to promote his ideas?

Koupal: His inventive mind constantly played with new voices and novel methods of getting his message across. At that time he wrote, "Barnum was right when he declared the American people liked to be deceived."

Defender: But didn't Baum ever reveal overt animosity toward American Indians, other than in these editorials?

Koupal: No, after the two *Pioneer* editorials he never expressed this view again throughout his long writing career. In February of 1890, Baum had called tolerance "the key to success in our country. It is this spirit which has won for us the name of being the most liberal and fair-minded among nations." He was focused on the Theosophists, who were committed to form a Brotherhood of Man, without distinction of race, creed, sex, caste, or color.

Defender: Then you would say a literal interpretation of the two editorials of Dec. 1890 and Jan. 1891 would be completely atypical of Baum's thinking as you understand it?

Judge: I object if you don't, Mr. Prosecutor. This guy has been leading *your* witness by the nose all the way. Sit down,

you public defending terrorist, and let's have a rousing redirect.

Prosecutor: Thanks a bundle, unkie. Ms. Koupal, this lowlife cynic has been gulling you into saying things that are not very helpful to our cause, which is, from the vantage of *now*, to protest straightforwardly the treatment of the Native Americans when it is politically lucrative to do so, and to attack L. Frank Baum for not doing it our way *then*. Now sit up straight and think hard. Can you think of anything Baum wrote later that even metaphorically might reveal his real feelings toward Native Americans?

Koupal: Well, in a 1906 Baum book *Mr. Woodchuck,* the following exchange appears between a Dorothy talkalike and a woodchuck: "She answered, 'when a woodchuck gets eating our clover and vegetables, we just have to do something to stop it. That's why my papa set the trap.'

'You're selfish,' said Mr. Woodchuck, 'and you're cruel to poor little animals that can't help themselves, and have to eat what they can find, or starve. There's enough for all of us growing in the broad fields.'" The woodchuck concluded that the land had "belonged to the wild creatures long before you people came here and began to farm."

Judge: Such arrant hostility! How do you figure that this stuff can possibly help our cause? Strike all of this counterproductive testimony. Hit the road, Koupal. And you, my idiot nephew, your next witness had better understand the way this system works, Sit down. I'm sending you back to Boalt for some remedial bonehead exercises when we're through with this case.

Prosecutor: Unk, could it be we got this all wrong? Maybe the truth lies elsewhere.

Judge: Adversarial! This is all about being adversarial! Truth has nothing to do with it. Who's next on your agenda?

Prosecutor: A round of applause for Thomas St. John, Green Mountain activist, waiting in the wings and rarin' to attack! This guy is the toprated sick 'em pitbull on our payroll. Front and center, Tom, old buddy.

Judge: Do you swear to screw the defendant, and no one but the defendant, so help you Yahweh?

St. John: I can do it on my head! Just ask me what I think about that genocidal maniac.

Judge: Your witness, Mr. Prosecutor.

Prosecutor: We already know about the incriminating editorials. What other bad things can you say about L. Frank Baum?

St. John: Baum advocated the extermination of the American Indian in his 1899 fantasy

"The Wonderful Wizard of Oz." The orphan Dorothy's violent removal from Kansas civilization, her enslavement to an evil figure – and the killing of this figure – these themes Baum takes from the already two hundred year old tradition of the Indian captivity narrative which stoked the fires of Indian-hating and its hope of "redemption through violence." The Wicked Witch of the West is illustrated in the 1900 first edition as a pickaninny, with beribboned, braided pigtails extended comically. Baum repeats the word "brown" in describing her. But this symbol's real historic depth lies in the earlier Puritans' confounding of European witches with the equally heathen American Indians.

Prosecutor: Who would have thought of that? A truly profound analysis! But give us some juicy details about Baum's Nazi suggestions about how to deal with the Indians. Whatever else have you unearthed?

St. John: Baum wrote *The Life and Adventures of Santa Claus* following the success of *The Wizard of Oz*. The illustrations in the book depict tomahawks, spears, hide-covered teepees, and the faces of Indian men, women, and children, fill the pages. Baum condemns the Awgwas, who represent Native Americans: "You are a transient race, passing into nothingness. We, who live forever, pity but despise you. On earth you are despised by all, and in heaven you have no place." After the "Great Battle Between Good and Evil," predictably enough, "all that remained of the wicked Awgwas was a great number of earthen hillocks dotting the plain." Baum is recalling newspaper photos of the burial field at Wounded Knee. The Wizard of Oz ruling his empire evokes the Imperial Wizard of the Ku Klux Klan. Baum's figure relates to the Jim Crow lynch law at the turn of the century.

Prosecutor: Can't ask for a more adept hatchet job than

that. Your gun is quick, and vengeance is yours! Your witness, Mr. Public Defender.

Defender: Mr. St. John, I defend to the steps of the guillotine your right to express your opinion that Baum's writings are elaborately constructed allegories. However, your arguments to support these interpretations are fair game for scrutiny and refutation. The Awgwas you refer to as Native Americans are described by Baum as semi-immortals of gigantic stature invisible to ordinary mortals, and able to fly swiftly through the air. The Master Woodsman and his allies vanquish the evil Awgwas and their cohorts the Asiatic Dragons, the three-eyed Giants of Tatary, the Black Demons from Patalonia, and the Goozle-Goblins. There is an illustration of the Master Woodsman after vanquishing this motley crew. He does have an ax (he *is* a woodsman, you know), but no tepees, tomahawks or Indians are anywhere in view. You are correct about

one thing: there is a color plate of what appear to be poor Indian children happily dancing later on in this book. Baum's textual reference to this scene can only be described as sympathetic to their plight. Did you read the book? Are you blind? These are the only two pictures in the volume that relate to the depictions that you concoct. I hereby submit these pictures as EXHIBIT B.[iii] Do you happen to recall the chronological relationship in the book between the defeat of the Awgwas and the reference to the "Indians?" Is it not true that the latter pacific images and the accompanying text do not appear until four chapters after the defeat of the Awgwas? These Awgwas have absolutely nothing to do with Indians, either literally or metaphorically. Therefore, Mr. St. John, you are either recklessly careless or simply lying to make a point, trusting that no one who reads your diatribe would have access to what is a relatively arcane book in the Baum literature. Thank you,

Mr. St. John, for your helpful testimony. You appear to be providing me with ammunition to prove my thesis. You might have made an honest reference to the "casual, unconscious racism"[iv] that surfaces in his "Sugarloaf Mountain" tale describing some hapless sugarloafers as composed "of sugar so dark in color that ... these folk seemed of less account than any of the others." But Mr. Baum is not on trial for "casual, unconscious racism." Your honor, I don't know who's paying this guy, but it's not me. St. John's theories are so cockeyed that he sounds suspiciously like a *provocateur* witness.

Judge: All right, that does it. Bailiff, trot this contemptuous exlawyer off to the pokey. I'll start disbarment proceedings tomorrow. Nephew, have your wife Honeypot step up here to replace this Public Disgrace of a Defender. We'll have no mistrial here. Step up, my dear, the pay's not bad. You're excused, Tom.

Prosecutor: Nice work, unk. The prosecution calls to the stand Prof. Waller Hastings. "Reverse psychology," professor?

Hastings: I see little evidence that Baum's editorials were intended to be taken tongue in cheek. This was an easily forgotten episode in Baum's life that would have been unlikely to have drawn further discussion during his own lifetime, and the sense that it had to be seen satirically looks like a back-formation from modern attitudes.

Prosecutor: What about the allegation that Baum in fact indulged in satire frequently in his writings?

Hastings: Baum wrote a lot of satire in his newspaper, and the editorials don't look like the same sort of writing, nor are the editorials the venue where he chose to put his satire.

Prosecutor: No further questions.

Judge: Your witness, my dear.

Honeypot: Can't think of a thing he hasn't already answered, judgie.

Judge: Well spoken. Your terse elocution hit the bull's-eye. No more witnesses in sight. Your final argument, Mr. Prosecutor.

Honeypot: Jus' hol' on, judgerino! R'member, I get paid by th' hour. An' me disgraced pred'cessor lef' a dep'sition tape I can play an' get paid f'r 'n th' meantime.

Judge: OK, Honeypot. I can always throw it out if the jury wakes up and listens to it. Let the tape roll.

Honeypot: The defense calls on the dep'sition tape o' Reneau H. Reneau t' chew up some time an' clink some nickels in me piggybank.

Tape: Hi, everybody! I'm Reneau H. Reneau, here to express another point of view. Ms. Koupal has been cited as the foremost authority on Baum's Dakota career, and after scouring a couple of her books on the subject, I don't doubt it a bit, although other than the two editorials already discussed, I couldn't find any other citation from Baum's works that appeared to be flagrantly racist. To the contrary, every other LFB reference to Indians cited in both of Koupal's books is a plea for tolerance. And *Mr. Woodchuck*! A powerful metaphor is at work here, wouldn't you say? Indeed, the same message appears in the editorials themselves, but expressed in an ingenious way. Take into account where Baum was at the time he wrote them? Absolutely! He was a reallyreally rad dude. Just read *Our Landlady*, where irony is a recurring device. And then read the offending editorials. Each was written not prior to but following a particularly brutal attack on the Indian people by the U.S. government, and they reek with *sarcasm*; they are beyond irony. They don't need scholarly interpretation. They really do speak for themselves. Their intent leapt at me because of my own experience with *provocateur* journalism or more generically, reverse psychology, Back in 1953 while a student at Berkeley and as an advocate of leniency for Julius and Ethel Rosenberg, I wrote an editorial for the *Oxford Accent* entitled "Kill the Rosenbergs," expounding the hardline point of view as obnoxiously as possible, the point being to generate sympathy for the contrary position. While my sassy foray may have had some imperceptible influence among the local population, I came to realize that only those who knew me pretty well appreciated my intent. This was ratified later with a letter to the Washington Post on another subject, and I never ventured further into the treacherous waters of *provocateur* journalism out of a vain but practical concern for my own reputation. Thrice burned, never

learned? Let's cut our losses. I note that Baum apparently came to the same conclusion. Unfortunately or fortunately for him, every word he ever wrote is still subject to scrutiny and judgment. And I respectfully suggest that unbending literalism in the interpretation of these two editorials is not only unfair to Baum, but completely misses his point. He was not advocating holocaust, he was *deploring* it, at the moment it was occurring, and in the midst of it. He was braver than any of us. READ THE WORDS OF BAUM FOR YOURSELF AND THEN DECIDE. THEY'RE IN THE BACKMATTER OF THIS BOOK. You just don't get it, my well-meaning friends. You are casting stones at an early advocate for Indian rights who found himself surrounded not by bloodthirsty redskins, but rather by his subscribers, bloodthirsty frontier rednecks. He made an heroic effort to defuse the tension in a way befitting a wordsmith equipped with psychological talent. Repent, ye latterday literalists! The gates of atonement are yet ajar!

Honeypot: Omigod, I w's blinker'd   an'   now   I panavis'alize! Judgiebunny, I move th' case against Baum be d'smissed due t' pr'pond'rance o' ev'dence in 'is favor!

Judge: Arouse thyself, burly bailiff, and awaken the peerless burgherkings in the jurybox. By the bowels of Yahweh I beseech ye all to forgive my myopic arrogance. I was one wrongheaded magistrate! The case is dismissed. May ye R. In Peace, L. Frank Baum.

---

[i] Ed. Note: the complete text of Baum's editorials appears in the Backmatter of this book.
[ii] *Mother Night* by Kurt Vonnegut, Jr. (Dell, 1961)
[iii] Ed. Note: Exhibit A and the Awgwa drawing (of Exhibit B) appear in Backmatter, while the dancing Indian children are the frontispiece of this article.
[iv] Katharine M. Rogers, introduction to *The Twinkle Tales* by L. Frank Baum (Univ. of Nebraska Press, 2005)

The Torquasian Times

Paris Picks A Veep!

For months now the supermarket press has trumpeted Ms. Hilton's *dynamite* announcement that she would be a candidate for the highest office in the US of A. Today she revealed she will partner with Janet Jackson on a star-power ticket. Disdaining traditional parties as "boring," the two hotties disclosed that their Wet 'n' Wild Party, abetted by the sizzling speed of the internet, has already qualified for the November ballot. The Dream Duo quickly captured the imagination of a jaded nation with their sassy slogan, "What you see is what you get." The stock market roared to unprecedented (See Paris Picks, P. 8A)

A Brand New Country
Th' Sultanate o' th' Godfearin' Land o' Goshen t' be Inaugurated T'day

The United Nations announced today that the Latest Kid on the Block, the Godfearin' Land o' Goshen, has been officially recognized and permitted to do business as a sovereign enterprise tied to the IMF and the World Bank, landing a chair on the U.N. Security Council Little is officially known about this Lilliputian isle with Gargantuan clout awash in the South Seas. Even the Sultan himself has yet to make a public appearance, although it is known that he is an especially generous sultan with regard to charities favored by those who recognize and otherwise promote his as yet unmapped island realm. The Secretary General has declared tomorrow to be a world holiday, and all world hostilities will be suspended pending ceremonies in the Holy City of Jerusalem where it is rumored that the Sultan may actually make his debut. All world leaders are expected to attend this (See Godfearin', P. 2)

God reveals that He does not exist

In a boggling revelation from Vatican City, an exchange between the Pope and the erstwhile Almighty was made public, where "God" admitted to being just another humbug. "I'm a Spaceguy from Aquarius with a Bag of Tricks," he stated to an amazed Pontiff. "I don't know what we're doing here any more than you do, but I had a good run. I really pulled it off, me gaudy peacock," the exDeity purportedly bragged to his ambassador on earth. The Pope today announced he would take over the duties of the now vacant office. "Somebody's got to be in charge," he explained to a bewildered universe, "and I've been rehearsing for this role all of my (See God, P. 9A)

The Bugby Legacy

"Ifay Iay amay eadingray isthay
essagemay ithoutway orization-
authay, aymay ymay oatthray
ebay utcay rossacay, ymay
onguetay orntay outay ybay
ethay ootsray, anday ymay

odybay
ebay uriedbay
inay ethay
oughray andsay
ofay ethay
easay."

AARGH!!

Egad!

Grease up your cash register, loyal Mystic Nit, you're about to take off on a venture into adventure capitalism that will oblige the U.S. Mint to schedule overtime for printing TwentyBuck bills and outsource the printing of C-Notes just to keep up with the demand that eager customers, dazzled by the charisma of your merchandise, are mailing to you in a neverending ratatat. The sheer weight of the cash in the ArmoredCars that are hauling away your DailyTake will have their axles breaking down before they can get to the bank.

Getting folks to want something they don't need is known as *marketing.* All Great Universities have BizAd Wizzmeisters hawking this holymoley to wideeyed catechumens. But you don't need an MBA to sell something. Here in a nitshell is the essence of "marketing:" **what counts is illusion, not product**. *We'll beat anyone's advertised price or your mattress is FREE.* Now that you know this, you can print out your MBA degree and stick it on the fridge.

Look around you and take note. The businessmen you know are actually involved in selling something that they have to keep in warehouses and sell either in stores or on the Internet, and they have to deal with abused items. They must hire an army of salesfellas who constantly require pumping up. They deal with klutzy warehousers who sweat, grunt, drop boxes on their toes and sue the company. At the end of the day these stressed-out moguls hardly have enough to pay the gas bill.

Sit up and quit picking your nose. You can rake in billions with none of that unseemly hassle. Follow me down the Path of Green to a MoneyMarket Monopoly! You can literally run the business from a yacht in the South Pacific. *This baby will change its own diapers.*

Ye may have heard it winkingly stated that a franchise for MacDonald's is a License to Print Your Own

Money. But I say unto you that this is far from a hahaha conceit; printing your own money when you need it is NOT a joke. Governments do it all the time, and so can you. "How?" you may ejaculate. The same way they do. You invent a unique name for your currency, say, "Nitbucks." Then you convince folks who exchange their sweat for printed paper with a distinguished name like "GreenBackaDolla" that they want to swap some DeadPresidents for Nitbucks. To do this you have to come up with some kind of desirable commodity that is available only with Nitbucks. Forget about the "Better Mousetrap;" that's claptrap. Come up with something you don't have to stack on pallets, *and get folks in Kansas to think they want it.* Then let them know it's readily available with Nitbucks. This strategy will metastasize your "product" throughout the known cosmos.

A revered precedent comes to noggin: the *Gift Certificate,* good only at the venue of the folks that print it. Of course the Big Winner in this transaction is the issuer of the piece of paper, which you cannot bank or indeed do anything with other than "spend" it at the issuer's place of business, some time in the future. Of course you can always give it away. But you can't redeem it for cash, nor do you get any change back if your purchase is less that the value stated on the certificate. And, too, there's always the possibility that you might lose it. The business might even bellyup before you get there; although it's hard to imagine that happening if this savvy entrepreneur turns enough tricks with his FunnyMoney. In other words, the *Gift Certificate* is in contention for the Guinness Most Lucrative Shellgame. garland .[1]

_____

[1] A more consumer friendly alternative comes to mind: casino chips, minted by the house to enhance security and expedite the parting of fools and their money. These colorful plastic discs can actually be redeemed for cash, if the suckers have any of them left after an evening of everything-

Enough of this banter-about-the-bush. *The bush is burning!* **The Oracle of Yahweh speaks!**. IF YOU ARE THE MYSTIC NIT TO WHOM THIS MISSIVE IS DIRECTED: HA HA HA. SINCE YOUR INDUCTION DECADES AGO WE HAVE SWINDLED YOU, SIMPLETON. We fed you doodly and milked your squat of all your life savings. You are now homeless, bereft of fortune and shorn of sacred honor.

So now for the good news, **TA DA !** Precisely because of your depraved loyalty you have been nominated to occupy a position in the highest ranks of Nitory – a seat on the Mystic Nit StarChamber of Commerce. No, this is not SPAM SPAM SPAM nor a fraud of any heritage at all. The StarChamber members that run the MysticNit hornswoggle can't reproduce fast enough to fill the new positions created by the demand

stays-on-the-reservation sin and games.

for our services, so we have to recruit from the ranks of the losers. You were selected because you have proven yourself to be as degenerate as you are destitute. In recompense for a Job welldone, we are offering you the fasttrack from LOSER To WINNER. And we're not talking 14,000 sheep, 6,000 camels, 1,000 yoke of oxen and 1,000 she asses. NONE OF THE ABOVE. You are being promoted from the disgusting ranks of the EXPLOITED to the blessed strata of the EXPLOITER. Advance from sheep to sheepherder and fleece the flock! A GOLDEN PASSPORT TO MAJESTY BEYOND HYPERBOLE. NitTrained Clearheads will be knocking at your barndoor to assist you in the transition.

POACHERS BEWARE: If somehow this document has fallen into the hands of an unwashed unNit or worse, an exNit apostate, HO HO HO! Your jig is over. The pages of this directive are impregnated with extract of poison ivy and

YOU AREN'T WEARING THE RUBBER GLOVES furnished to the legitimate addressee that protected him from imminent and ghastly death throes. As you die, these papers will burst into flame from the acid in your sweat, destroying all evidence. What? This is a bloody copy of the original and therefore impregnation free? Well, so what. HO HO HO again, loser. The ANCIENT CURSE[2] appearing at the outset of this tiptop secret document will take care of you with hours of angst and agony thrown in, and evidence be damned. It is useless to attempt to outmaneuver a Master Mystic Nit.

---

[2] The alert reader will note that this Ancient Curse appears to be in some dialect of PigLatin. This unpopular language, invented by the OSS during WW II to confound enemy "intelligence" (ha ha) is diabolical in its simplicity – and it continues to foil even the most senile and unwary among us. Research has uncovered variants of this spooky tongue: *Ifyay Iyay amyay eadingray isthey ookbay...* and then there's *aymay ymay oatthray ebay utcay acrossway...*Simon Elron's careful analysis reveals that the primary difference between these competing dialects seems to be the use of either the consonant "w" or the "y" before the standard igPay atinLay suffix "ay." Usage, or "the market," however, rejects the need for any unnecessary consonant whatsoever, and it is to the dictates of the proletariat (the "market") that we genuflect in our own prefatory rendition. Controversy surrounds the evolution of igPay atinLay's grammatical structure. Does it tend to appeal to the eye (as written medium) or the ear (spoken)? Methinks the eyes don't have it. Anyways, here's a challenge to the reader: come up with an igPay atinLay "Elements of Style" of your own as an exercise in linguistics. Not as easy as it sounds/looks, eh? What about those pesky single syllable words? Diphthongs? Silent consonants? Weird articulations? Et cetera? OodGay uckLay. Zamenhof, the Great and Terrible Oculist of Byalistok, struggled with this challenge for a stretch, producing a Frankenstein concoction that after roaming the wastelands for over a century has yet to come up with a palatable *bon mot*. Here's what our terrifying curse looks like in ZamenhofSpeak: *Se mi estas leganta ĉi tiu libro rajigo, povus mian gorĝon esti distranĉ, mia lingvo ŝirita for de la radikoj, kaj mia korpo esti entombigita en la malglata sasblo de la maro.*

So now it's gobblegobble time, turkeylurkey. We have ambitious plans for you. You must first acquire a country. You have three options. You can (a) buy it (b) rent it or (c) conquer it. Unless you have a secret weapon or an Isle of Monte Cristo stashed away somewhere you can forget about doing any of these things on your own. But now of course you can count with the mighty backing of the Mystic Nit StarChamber of Commerce! We have unheard-of clout that will propel you to dominion over your own chunk of RealEstate. From this day forward cash flow will be from the Mystic Nit treasury to YOU. Not like heretofore, wot? We will provide you with the muscle and the *consiglieri* to keep you accelerating toward the real objective: CONTROL OF THE PLANET. Of course, we will be your partners in this megenterprise. You would hardly want to spend you days shrugging around like Atlas, now would you? There is no

possibility of your refusing this offer. I shudder to contemplate the consequence of any intimation of negativity. I am watching you RIGHT NOW. If you accept, with great zest rub your stomach, pat the top of your head, and wink your right eye. If you refuse, don't do any of those things, or do them with anything less than exuberance and trust that Yahweh is more merciful than I am, ha ha ha. We already signed Him up with an offering of the firstlings of our flock and of the fat thereof. What you got for Him, loser? Peas and carrots? There; that's settled.

Your assignment will encompass the three classic stages of any successful protocol for world domination: **(1) Setup (2) Operation and (3) Exit Strategy.** We'll briefly discuss each step.

(1) Setup. Initially we will provide you with a sultanate and anoint YOU as Sultan. All we need is a rock in the ocean which you can officially use as an address for pomp, circumstance, and commercial enterprise, unhampered by nuisance ordinances and taxes. Of course, any actual work involved in the business we propose for you will be outsourced to coolies. We will in fact rent the country (option "b," if you recall) from some Micronesiac *führer* who would welcome deriving any income at all from a nuisance in his bay. We will make sure that the lease specifically includes sovereign rights during your tenure, and we will insist upon a treaty with the tyrant to guarantee his protection in the event of any external threat. We will then construct a fortress on the rock, which will serve as your WhiteHouse in the event of any official government bash. Of course, we don't plan anything of the sort, attuned as we are to efficiency in government, but other installed potentates may expect this expensive perk as an excuse for "doing business," and we've got to accommodate those bastards. Somebody might show up, and we'll have

to keep up appearances, so *the cellar will be stocked with casks of Amontillado*. The fortress will be staffed by a teetotalin' couple from Kansas. The Whitehouse of your monarchy will be powered by Oceanenergy™ and duly fitted with cuttin' edge Lighthouse appointments. We will name your country "Th' Godfearin' Land O' Goshen," and announce that your official Federal Constitution is the Ten Commandments. You can even announce ready-to-go amendments that declare gay parades to be unconstitutional, and spittin' on the flag o' Goshen to be a capital crime. That'll buy you good press even from the Taliban. All governments prosper from the culture o' morality, which saves lots o' money otherwise heavily invested in security for the Second Estate and its cronies, leaving more GNP available to cover the social responsibilities of the NRA.[3] *La proprieté est*

---

[3] Firstclass NRAers need to stockpile gold and guns for the eventual world class war. WMDs are appropriate for

le vol? (property is theft). Just another French *bon mot.*[4] All business will be transacted by you and your crew via Internet and cell phone from your yacht somewhere in the South Seas.

(2) Operation. At the gitgo, your nation's economic activity will consist entirely of Internet gambling, and Goshen will become the MonteCarlo o' CyberSpace. All transactions will be conducted with Nit-

_____

the NRA neo-aristocrats who can afford them. However, the Saturday Nite specialists, with their national riflettes, generally use them against each other. Only *chusma* shoot each other for motives other than profit. Excellent riddance.

[4] All French Lit is just one big *plaisanterie*, me *singe méchant*. An early example is the Great Riddle of Charlemagne: *Qu'un monsieur fait-il le fait de se lever, une dame s'assoyant et un chien sur trois jambes? Réponse:Ils lisent Sartre. (Le faut de charrier juste! La réponse réele est "serrent les mains.")* Loose translation: What does a man do standing up, a woman sitting down and a dog on three legs? Answer: Read Sartre. (Just kidding! the real answer is "shake hands.")

bucks, purchased by credit/debit cards from -- where else? -- the Godfearin' Bank o' Goshen. The only thing that can be purchased with Nitbucks is of course participation in virtual gaming activity, although Nitbucks may be redeemed for Green-BackaDollas at any time. *No problema.* This generates CONFIDENCE in our INTEGRITY. Naturally, no shame will be spared in an effort to decelerate redemptions by making our virtual roulette as exciting and sensual as prudent prurience may permit, with playbunnies spinning the wheels of chance. Initially, ALL income will be redistributed to your clients as gambling winnings, that is, your *take amount*[5] will be zero. Op-

_____

[5] *Take amount* being that portion normally kept back from the gross for taxes (we won't have any), expenses, and profit. What remains is then distributed as winnings. Usually this "take amount" doesn't exceed 25%. Say we've got a heads-or-tails booth where you bet a buck on heads or tails. While the probability of a winning toss is even (.5, or 1 out of

erating costs will be sustained by advertising revenue. This gives you an EDGE over the competition. Advertising enhances the CREDIBILITY of our enterprise. It translates to "Goodwill" in the assets column. The Treasury of the Nit-Star Chamber will be tapped to publicize the virtues o' Goshen's official website, **holymoley.com**. Professional spamgushers will blog all over the net. Free, albeit nonconvertible, Nitbucks will be deposited in courtesy Nitbuck bank accounts opened for key MoverShakers throughout the globe. The din o' the trombone o' fanfare will escape no livin' earbone.

When a peak o' frenzied **buzzbang!** has been attained, and the big winners have been identified and publicized[6], we will launch a second activity, related to the first, but this one is blessed with megapotential. The *real faces* of the Delirious who actually Win Something comprise the very linchpin of this enterprise. You will flash around the globe the Grins o' the Few, the Happy Few, the Band o' Winners! Governments are notoriously reluctant to let the Free Market mess around with this juicy business. They brook no competition: it's a funfunfun regressive tax: we're talkin' LOTTERY, good buddy.[7] Of

---

2) you wouldn't expect to get $2 for a winning flip, would you? $1.60 is more like it. As the probability of your winning decreases, the payout increases, but it never will reflect actual probability, not if the Mafia expects to maintain its lavish lifestyle. If you paid $1 to guess the card pulled at random from a full deck of cards, how much would you expect to win if you called it? Somewhere around $40 is probably the answer.

---

[6] All entrants will be asked to sign waivers entitling you to exploit their faces and spam around their scripted interviews in the event of a successful run, with no additional remuneration. At this early stage, no one will refuse to sign this endorsement; in fact it will serve to further animate your customers until their bank accounts are drained.

[7] Yes, *Lottery,* not *Sweepstakes.* They're not the same thing. Tradi-

course we've got our own government and we make our own laws, don't we? And the Internet is wide open, at least for now. We're talkin' Babe, the Big Green CashCow, and we'll milk 'er till 'er teats turn blue. You know, a curious thing happens on the route to milliondollar payoffs. The probability of winning is so pitifully retarded that for any given contender it's effectively braindead. Someone has calculated that the chances of winning the California Super Lotto Plus jackpot is one in forty-one million, four-hundred sixteen thousand, three-hundred fifty-three. Note that putting it that way doesn't really discourage anybody, and that's why we could care less when all the DoGooders cite these irrefutable odds[8]. Why would anyone

squeeze his sweat into this pit? You know the answer, me feisty puppy. Because he's mesmerized by those HAPPY FEW who actually HIT THE POT. They're bragging all over TV about how they're going to SPEND IT. *Bejabbers, those bastards look just like we do, or like somebody we know, or at least like somebody!* Your Cosmic NitLottery will be the **Darling** of the *Consumer Reports* **Best-Bet Derby**, the FastTrack to Fat-City.[9] Painted on Page One of every tabloid, every blog on the bugbog planet, are those SmileyFaces of MerryWinners -- your neighbors, friends of your neighbors, cousins of friends of your neighbors --

---

tionally, lotteries require an entrance fee, and sweepstakes usually do not.
[8] If every possible lottery combination were to be written on a slip of paper and dropped into a Really Big Hat, and if every breathing soul in California: babes, kids, buzzin' cousins, grandpas, illegals, et cetera, each were to draw a single slip, there

would STILL be slips in the hat. Hell, let every livin' mutha (i.e. *everybody*) in Nevada, Idaho and New Mexico each draw one of the remaining slips. There'd STILL be slips in the hat. And remember, only ONE slip matches the jackpot. You can see why my *sobrino* calls the *lotería* the *impuesto* of the *tarugos*.

[9] Of course, winners will be demographically determined according to rigorous marketing mantra.

generating tidal waves of new NitLotterers!

(3) Exit Strategy. Even "Honest" Abe, phrasemonger of legend, admitted that be they blue or be they gray, or any other hue that may, he couldn't fool *all* the ninnies *every* day, hey hey! Time for the master heist, me greedy piggy.

We will now invest in blackmarket state-o'-th'art Weapons o' Mass Destruction, the newfangled nanochip models that are impossible to detect. Now's the moment to scuttle the ship o' state, but we'll exit with the grand gesture. On the Godfearin' Land o' Goshen Stock Exchange (an icon on your desktop) *we go public with the NitLottery!* Investors worldwide will hock their socks[10] for a piece o' the action. We'll bribe Coalitions o' th' Willin' (they need hard cash), install our WMDs to surround every form of life, and leave our army o' investors with a fistful o' Nitbucks

---

[10] MBAers say "leverage the ranch."

and a rented rock in the bay, while we assume control of every bank in the Yellow Pages. You then sail off into the sunrise and leave the doughty couple from Dodge to meet the press.[11] The Bankers, the Enforcers, are now us. Any objections? *Ye are the anointed frontman.*

Negotiate your airfare to Providence, R.I. at once. Email your flight info along with any comments and suggestions to: *sticnitsmyav@olymoleyhay.com.* And above all, be sure to encrypt everything into igPayat-inLay and confound the spooks. You will be met at the airport there by a trusted Nit who will be hopping discreetly on his left foot and patting his patootie. You will countersign by doing a quick pushup and throwing your hat at the security guard. Our contact man will then pay off the security

---

[11] With a little neogothic imagination it might occur to our Jayhawkers to open up the cellar for their inquiring guests, who notoriously have a penchant for lubrication, then quietly sneak out the back and swim ashore.

guy and escort you to our underground headquarters, where you will be groomed for your mission. Get goin'. The Force is your pal. We are the world.

BACKMATTER

Notes and Bibliography

The Great Battle Between Good and Evil

*From "The Life and Adventures of Santa Claus"
by L. Frank Baum, 1902*

*IF **HE** DIDN'T, WHO DID? commentary*

It is impossible not to sympathize with a father justifiably outraged at the injustice of the justice system. The impact of his daughter's sobs when the verdict was read was overwhelming. That being said, Simon Elron's variation on the theme of *The Brentwood Murders* is presented here as an operatic fantasy. It is a callous blame-the-victim treatment of a contemporary tragedy, and it crashes through the boundaries of tasteless sensationalism, which is of course the point. I trust enough time has elapsed to permit this ghastly incident and subsequent events to be used as a backdrop for social commentary. As to why the jury could be so receptive to the golden tones of a cynical but skilful defense, I can refer you to an angry work, *White Like Me,* by Tim Wise (Soft Skull Press, 2004). And if you're interested in developing an honest working libretto (Paging Alice Goodman!), I believe Jeffrey Toobin's *The Run of His Life* (Random House, 1996) to be an objective account of the trial itself. This could be the "Peter Grimes" moment for John Adams. The (real) Simpson Trial has it all.

Simon Elron's creative version of the tragedy was derived from *Rigoletto, Traviata,* and of course, *Otello* (whose original Italian title was to be *Jago,* the Italian spelling of Iago). *Mefistofeles* and our very own *American Tragedy* (AKA *A Place in the Sun*) can likewise take a bow. The role of Yam Snosnibor? Google *Judith Regan* if you have any questions. In another classic instance of irony Johnny Cochran quoted Jas. Russell Lowell in his spellbinding "Truth forever on the scaffold" summation. The blood sweat & tears buzzline belongs of course to Winnie-the-Poo (he of #10 Downing).

Of course the circus and pompenstance of any justice system has already been relegated to Wonderland by Lewis Carroll as "just a pack of cards." Does justice exist? On my blipscreen it's just another figment cluttering perception. To "believe in justice" it is necessary to buy into the good-and-evil (read "right and wrong") theories that have been so wildly popular for centuries. Even so, *original sin* does appear to me to be closer to the mark than *blank slate*. "If good and evil don't exist, it's necessary to invent them," is a convenient saw that has been repeated by fat burghers who can't find any logical support for these notions but find them useful to make all those ragpickers feel guilty about not having enough to eat. In contrast, there is a theory that can claim some "scientific" lineage: the prospect that human behavior is simply a product of chemical reactions within the human brain. I urge you to check out some recent challenges to the whole notion of individual accountability. You can start with *The Nature Assumption* by Judith Rich Harris (Free Press, 1998), *Born That Way* by William Wright (Knopf, 1998), and *Living with Our Genes* by Dean Hamer and Peter Copeland (Anchor Books, 1999). While I recommend these books, in no way do I suggest that any of these straitlaced academics would subscribe to my own wild and crazy notions.

Pursuing the implications of chemical determinism we can derive explanations for those among us who flaunt social taboos, like pederasts or wifebeaters. The great majority of us haven't inherited any proclivity to engage in these activities – to the contrary, the very notion is a turnoff. A few ne'er-do-wells down the block possibly do harbor a hankering but are chemically equipped to repress it, while some of our less fortunate – or less blessed, if you prefer – fellow citizens apparently are programmed to succumb to the acid in their brains and damn the torpedoes. And most blokes in each category profess to believe in the good/evil dogma. Brainwashed by righteous tradition, many of them may even feel "guilt" for their iniquities, further plunging them into either denial and rebellion or depression and self-hatred. Not good. I hasten to add that while determinism banishes the smugness and hypocrisy associated with moral principle, it doesn't alter the need for social standards and law enforcement.

A Newer Theology

What? I'm anti-Semitic? Much, much more than that. I'm anti-Yahweh, anti-he hiding behind whichever of his thousand names. Yeah, I'm talkin' at you too, Allah Akbar. Hang on, folks, for a little revisionist theology. The War in Heaven between the Good and the Bad was actually won by the devil, who stripped God of his magic, went ahead with his own creationism, ghostwriting and publishing the "good" Book, deceiving everybody. Official history is always writ by the victor. Jesus of Nazareth? He was duped just like the rest of us, and look where it got *him*. This explains the contradiction, injustice, pain and suffering that we all experience, enthralled as we are by the Great Satan. What's that you say? "So what else is new?" Well, let's try out a more nuanced approach to this godolatry stuff. Let's assume that God has spelled out standards of conduct he presumably expects men to live by. Further we'll stipulate that free will exists, and everyone (except the legally insane) understands the difference between "right" and "wrong." Postgraduation awards/punishments will be meted out to each individual according to his/her performance. In addition, let's agree that this same deity included an anecdote in his Chronicles wherein he tells a devoted disciple to offer up his son as a burnt offering. This devout zealot is about to consummate the deed, but at the last minute an angelic emissary appears and says, "Never mind, you have just passed the 'fear of God' test, and here's a goat you can use instead." This seemingly innocuous account implies several things, but one is that in order to test your mettle, God may deceive you as to his own intentions and work in disingenuous ways. Perhaps this God published a giant Book of bullshit just to see how many of us could see through it. Those who, of their own free will, suck up to the bogeyman "God" depicted therein, in spite of their innate understanding of "right" and "wrong," will then be punished accordingly. This way I get the harp and Falwell gets the time out. Hey! Chill out, ol' buddy.

SO THIS IS ARCTURUS! _commentary_

The versatile Eidoideator entertains the prospect of a two hour _Dinner with André_ extended to millions of years. By the way, the three Eidoideator quotes, in order of appearance, are from _Leaves of Grass, Misanthropology,_ and the heralded _Book of Job_ {KJV}. That _ta da!_ business is lifted from the unheralded film _Galaxina,_ while "...you totally ain't no Isadora" is a reference to an apocryphal (?) interchange between George Bernard Shaw and Isadora Duncan. And all right, I'll admit that "who once held all Foggybottom atremble" was practically lifted verbatim from _Tosca._ The unappreciated bard who coined "talentgang" was e.e. cummings. GIGO is pretty standard lingo now for "garbage in, garbage out," the programmer's excuse for not screening the data he processes in his program. Kenneth Patchen, another great and underappreciated American pioneer, merits a round of applause for the _and begin again_ punchline See _Cloth of the Tempest,_ (Padell, 1958). The design of this book is itself a poem.

But isn't this getting to be a bit toomuch? Do you really need all this academic correctness? Doesn't it maybe look like I'm just another M. Jourdain preening pseudoerudition in your face? Send commentary and LettersTotheEditor c/o the _New York Times_, who majors in that stuff. Academic honesty interrupts the movement of narrative. If it's _interesting_, that's REALLY news, whether fact or fiction, of recent or antique vintage. The entire concept of plagiarism is absurd, wot? If it comes to mind and it works, stick it in, I say. Except for neologimmicks, every word ever uttered is plagiarism. Origins of words, sentences, and ideas make for an interesting pastime, providing grist for trivia game shows, and Google can help you out if you're inclined to pursue the genealogy of phrases. What resonates and still rings of veracity is worth repeating, not the name of who might have first coined or popularized it or something similar. The original utterer would be proud his notion marches on, if indeed he could recognize its evolved configuration. All of Emerson's best thoughts were stolen by the ancients, according to him. An obsession with attribution clogs the page with unsightly superscripts, footnotes, op. cits., and et cet. And notions of great pith and moment with this regard their currents turn awry, and lose the name of action. Remember, you first heard it here.

Compare and discuss *Ask not said John Kennedy what your country can do for you* (Ted Sorenson, 1961) to *Ask rather said warty bliggens what the universe has done to deserve me* (Don Marquis, 1927).

He dicho, as Cantinflas and so many others have said so many times in so many ways. *I know! I know!*

There, I digress again, sermonizing like my daddy used to do. Back to me job-at-hand. The five bonnie yarmulke game is a reworking of the "colored hat logic poser" presented by Martin Gardner as "Recreational Logic" in a 1961 masterful accomplishment *The Second Scientific American Book of Mathematical Puzzles and Diversions* (Simon and Schuster, 1961). Gardner points out the weakness of any solution at all to this problem, due to the questionable assumptions about level of astuteness and vagueness as to appropriate time lapse. The endpaper Riddle-Me-Rees are variations of Gardner puzzles. Here I go again, attributing, in spite of the prior paragraphs deploring the practice. I really do admire this venerable genius. He even stands tall beside Baum and Thompson with an Ozbook of his veryown (*Visitors from Oz*, St. Martin's Press, 1998) that includes an appropriate mathematical twister.

If the sexual orientation of Scaevola and Laya has been sorted out to your satisfaction, you can fastforward to the next paragraph. Muzio is a straight sort, way ahead of the herd in many,

many ways, but dotty in others. The Princess is a (male) transvestite, dotty in some ways and way, way ahead of the herd in others. Forgive me if I spell it out here clearly, loudly. I do think it's already writ large in the conversation itself, and this is just an innocent preemptive gesture in the unlikely event that you didn't get it. But don't feel badly if wasn't as obvious as I seem to be implying. Obsessed with being hip and hopefully waggish, I probably wouldn't have figured it out myself without the inside advantage. I should have made it clearer, perhaps, that Scaevola's "secret" of being a (female) transvestite was only the projection of a figment in Laya's subconscious mind.

One final comment on the games we might consider playing on our voyage from tick to tock. How about this one? Chess is presumably all strategy, with little intervention permitted for the gods of chance, depending on opponent's level of astuteness and anticipated reaction. Unrealistic, I say. Let's toss in some dice, to simulate honesttogod unpredictability, like the real world we infest. Craps and Monopoly come to mind. It's a simple notion. One die is presented to each player. It must be used before each play except for the following situations: the first two moves for both sides, and whenever (it will occur) either side finds itself in the embarrassing position of *check*. In these events, the die cannot restrict any legal move and is sidelined. It is required for all other moves, and only the piece determined by the toss of the die may then be moved. Any move other than the check-obliged may be waived, however, and the turn is forfeit. If the die signals a piece that cannot be moved, the turn is likewise lost. A snake eye is appropriately the King himself. A deuce is the Queen, second place as customary but the real power behind the scepter (DiddlyDick comes to mind). A trey summons the rook (castling included), a four the pusillanimous and beleaguered bishop, a fiver the foolhardy knight, and a boxcar – what's left? – the nonplussed sacrificial pawn, God love 'is expendable bum. It is rumored that this yuppie variation of a grizzled pasttime has been a great hit with the soccermoms of Orange County, who use it to while away sweltering hours in the bleachers while their kids duke it out on the playing fields of Anaheim.

MR. VICI FORGES A COALITION commentary

This is a continuation of "The Excelsior Odyssey," inaugurated in *Misanthropology: a Florilegium of Bahumbuggery,* seminal in the genre. Familiarity with the parent narrative is not prerequisite.

A Cosmogonical Theory

Once upon a time in the Great OutBack there was an Energetic Consciousness from WhoKnowsWhere that could think but not perceive (i.e. *eyeball*) anything in the dimension(s) it was privy to, because there was nothing there, or at least nothing it could sense. After playing mind games for what must have been a "long time," this Awareness got bored with games that were entirely of its own invention. No surprise, no challenge. It thoughtfully designed a solution to boredom involving selfdisintegration, but with seeds of regression planted to insure that its Original Consciousness would ultimately (timelength, whatever that means, of no concern) be restored, new and improved by interesting experience. So **kaboom!** and it was transformed into zilllions of semi-independent bits of consciousness. After extended tribulation it will return to its original state, wiser for the journey (run a modified newsreel in reverse, maybe?). I find some satisfaction in this concept.

The foregoing is the cosmic nugget mined by Lt. Snurl, ultimately adopted by Mr. Vici and discussed in this narrative in the Vici/Cavinu dialog. Spicing up this lively conversation is a rehash of that old bugaboo, time itself. TIME: a classroom exercise in interpreting revolving arrows or flashing glyphs on the wall that has spawned an obsolescenceproof gadget industry. No one, however, has been able to pin down exactly what it is. These and other exciting paradoxes would ultimately become the Garden of Main Ideas in *Bionosis, the Art of Autodelusion*, but that's another saga.

During the DarkAges of academia at Berkeley (era of Bob Sproul and the Loyalty Oath) and just prior to the dawn of the New Renaissance, I was a resident at Oxford Hall, a student co-op and multiethnic oasis in the fratcampus desert. The motleycrue therein residing did cryptically anoint me as more likely to succeed at the cosmology game than at anything else. Need I add that I learned more from these guys than from the loyalty-certified faculty? I have therefore taken seriously the challenge, and the chronicle before your eyes sums up my musings on that subject, ever ticking away in my mindfield and now ready for the booming. First of all let me make clear that I'm not promoting any notion. I solicit no convert. I only report to you my observations, *como diablo viejo*, after a century (more or less) of looking around and within, and trust that you will at least find them interesting. I don't "believe" what I say myself; I just think it worthy of consideration. However, the notion proposed by Lt. Snurl seems to me one plausible explanation of our present "what th'?" condition. I'm sorry, but the idea of worshiping any "God" just makes no sense to me at all. I would rather think that we ourselves may be tiny slivers of this "God," and if pride is a deadly sin, selfadulation must be even deadlier. Who would dare to attribute "pride" to his morally upright God?

Ramblings on Evildom

Consider for a moment images of *de jure* EvilDoers. I'm talking drunks, child molesters[1], and Nazis. In my lifetime all of the above have been subjected to demonization and bad press. But hey! No need to badmouth anybody, including even Geo. W. Bush, who in the first place would never have been in a position to wreak or havoc anything without the connivance of people like us. We the burghers in order to achieve a more inequitable distribution of earth treasure do hereby for the histories our surrogates write for us award prizes for eloquence to those who are successful in advancing our perceived interests and massaging our selfesteem. We hang upsidedown those who are not good at this, which may eventually be the fate of El Dubya, just like Il Duce. I'd be the first to rush to the defense of this *pobre diablo*, who after all is just our elected yes elected anything else is denial patsy. Our representatives whether chosen, anointed, or by *coup d'etat*, have no more clue than do we. They're just HeatResistant, as a callous Queen of Hearts recently demonstrated while burning cookies in the kitchen during a run for HighOffice.

---

[1] OK, now that we're all relaxed and drunk with let-the-id-do-the-talking camaraderie, let's trespass into taboo. For the nth time I aver that I'm not advocating anything, I'm just telling you what it looks like to me after 75 years. I dont care if you agree with me or not, but I hope you do grant me the opportunity to speak my mind before you cancel your subscription. I think the child molester is getting a bad rap and the children involved are being severely crippled by the ignorance of parents and community. At the time of molestation, if no violence is involved, isn't it possible that the child may be confused, but certainly not traumatized, any more than he would be if he saw a poor old woman swallow a fly? The unsensational explanation could be given to the child that this behavior is unacceptable, and the perpetrator is indeed an oddball and should receive statesponsored training. No trauma would occur if it were left at that. The psychodamage occurs with the uncontrollable outrage of people like us and the complicity of inquisitional preachers and psychologists who make a comfortable living by spinning mass hysteria.

<u>Interruptions to Flow of Narrative</u>

Sources of quotations follow, as required in the name of ACADEMIC HONESTY according to Prof. Judy Hunter (to whom "Attention Must Be Paid!") of Grinnell College, in her Advice for Students on Citation and Scholarship (Google it).

"Let them eat *caca!*" is a steal from Ma. Antoinette, who purportedly put it this way: "*Qu'ils mangent de la brioch.*" Sounds callously witty, but in context she might have meant something a dumb French blonde would really say.

"The enemy of my enemy" is a restatement of Bin/BushLadin logic. I like to think I have a finetune here.

The concept that alcohol is a source of energy for robots was derived from the dazzling TV series *Futurama,* and might explain the canny wisdom of the series hero, Bender, ironically the unlikely model for our own uncanny Lt. Snurl.

Robert A. Heinlein, an unadmired martinet, nonetheless was a good SciFi wordsmith. "Harsh Mistress" is his invention, in his case referring to our own moon. Al Capp, of Li'l Abner comic immortality, created the character J. Colossal McGenius, who charges for advice by the word. I just adjusted his rate for inflation. Capp can also take credit for Adam Lazonga, Ol' Man Mose, Kickapoo Joy Juice, and of course Pansy Yokum and her visions.

The Univac Larc ("Cral Cavinu"), or the Livermore Advanced Research Computer, perhaps the world's first supercomputer, was installed in the Lawrence Radiation Laboratory. At the time, I, a lowly Univac I[2] operator and

---

[2] Founding Father of the race. Univac I, of 1,000 memory positions, required an onsite refrigerator bigger than the CPU along with live-in engineers to keep running. The fulltime operation course was of 16 weeks duration. I recall the tour guide explaining to concerned visitors that Univac was just a speedy idiot that could be programmed to master the strategy of TicTacToe because all possible move combinations could be stored in its memory, but could never be "taught" to play a good game of chess, which requires on-the-spot reaction to a

instructor at the Census Bureau, never actually saw it. We in Suitland, Md. did refer to this Goliath on the other ocean in hushed tones, and eventually got to see its younger bro at the David Taylor Model Basin. (Honestly, by this time awash in Univacs, I was more impressed by the model basin itself).

"That's my story and I'm sticking to it," trademark remark of a latterday Irish wit, Colin Quinn. Injustice? Adam Sandler, heir to Shemp and Moe, gets boxoffice thumbsup, while understated wit in the Martin Mull tradition plays to a discriminating coterie of appreciators, with disproportionate remuneration. I do digress.

Reducing 70% of humanity to a pinpoint in the circuitry of a robot is a drastic solution to a real problem. I suggest that overpopulation is devastating the planet, and relying on warfare to thin out the population is barbarous. Less radical solutions are available. There is that parable of Jimmy and Ginny, kindergarten kids who approach their teacher and announce their plans to get married. "Have you considered the consequences? How could you afford to care for your children?" the practical pedagogue asks. "We've already thought about that," says Jimmy. "Every time Ginny lays an egg I'll step on it." Or in grandam Nancy parlance, if the pill doesn't work, just say "abort."

For the Grand Finale to the brief blip of the bugbogger tribe on the screen of life, I really tried to get permission to reprint the dream of the ardent young Nazis in *Cabaret*, those ironic lyrics to *Tomorrow Belongs to Me*, but no permit forthcame. All of us are Nazis, of course. Too many of us are Nazi hawks, ripping out the livers of those we perceive as a threat to our ideals. Most of us are temperate burghers who *heil,* look the other way, and then divvy up with the hawks the plunder we have amassed. Too few of us are "good" Nazis. Anyway, *God Save the Queen* requires no reprint rights and gets the job done, don't you agree.

---

myriad of possibilities, and an evolving strategy. The visitors were reassured, and laughed uneasily.

#*@#!! commentary

George Van de Wetering was my Jr. yr. English teacher at Santa Cruz High School. A lefty intellectual during the era of Joe McCarthy, he dedicated his talents to challenging his students to tune in to Great Literature and develop a point of view. Gros is a character loosely patterned after Ira Wallach's Luke in "God's Little Best Seller," (*Hopalong Freud Rides Again*, Henry Schuman, 1952). Uncle Don still lives in legend today due to an incident that apparently never happened. Prattlers still blog about "your old Uncle Don," thinking the mike was off at the end of his kiddie radio program, sneering "that should hold the little bastards." Anyway his progeny should revel in the legend. Otherwise Uncle Don would be in the dustbin.

The North's relationship with the South today proves how talking with one's perceived adversary could have proven to be mutually beneficial, in stark contrast to the violent convulsion invoked by that brooding, ubiquitous E. Pluribus Abe. In fairness to him, all "great" presidents, queens, lord protectors and potentates have painfully sacrificed their peons on the altar of blood. It is thus that they achieve statue-status in the eyes of the lords and ladies, their poets laureate, and ultimately the tribe itself.

There is a reason why *misanthropology* is the theme proclaimed in the cynical rants chronicled herein. I'm leveling with you here, putting into perspective what I observe, without necessarily identifying myself with any of the folks who do all the ranting. I've learned that "reverse psychology" works just as well when attributed to fictional characters. Let *them* take the heat from those who don't get it. Look carefully: it's not me talking most of the time. I'm just an innocent paparazzo plyin' me trade. A vet and a senior citizen, yet. My own P.O.V. has wobbled around over the years, so I can't claim to be certain or zealous about anything at all. I have no incentive to convince anyone of anything. Consistency hobgoblins not my little mind. Just the urge to throw some notions at the wall and see what sticks. So call off your swiftboaters and waterboarders, DiddlyDick. I never thought you'd notice. Write a book, rather, about your own neophilosophy.

THE PERILS OF SATIRE commentary

This is an update on the *Misanthropology* essay "The Yellow Brick Trail of Tears," where Baum's Indian editorials are subjected to a revisionist interpretation. The following characters in this essay are strawmen/haywomen invented by me to support my thesis: Prosecutor, Defender, Judge Rambo Dredd, and Honeypot. The words in their mouths I have put there to serve my pronounced end. All others in the drama are real names and real people. The words attributed to them are either true-to-context quotations or libelproof honest summaries of their statements, either in published material or in emails to me. Insight into Baum's thinking at the time of the editorials is provided by Nancy Tystad Koupal in two fascinating compilations with extensive commentary, *Baum's Road to Oz – the Dakota Years* (South Dakota State Historical Society Press, 2000) and *Our Landlady* (University of Nebraska Press, 1996). The introduction to "Perils" was reprinted from the latter volume. The format of the "trial" is of course dialectic. I must admit I wonder at times if I'm not flailing at strawpeople myself in my stubborn insistence in pursuing this crusade. In spite of sympathetic reviews in the Baum Bugle, Oz fans appear to be generally unconcerned about the controversy, as though to say, "No matter. We could care less about his politics. Baum wrote some really inspired worldclass stuff for kids, and that's what we celebrate. We like Oz precisely because it transports us to a nonpolitical world."

A zero tolerance policy towards anything proclaims its own intolerance, and thus compromises its own justification. My hypothetical letter-to-the-editor here attempts, as an exaggerated example, through *reverse psychology* to promote the notion that any policy of zero tolerance can be expensive and counterproductive. As to *In the Court of Public Opinion*, it was the title of a book by Alger Hiss as his defense against charges of espionage and perjury.

Satire is the use of ridicule and sarcasm to expose or attack perceived folly and injustice. In his Indian editorials, Baum writes, "And these, his conquerors, were marked in their dealings with his people by selfishness, falsehood, and treachery. What wonder that his wild nature, untamed by years of subjection, should still revolt?"

Sarcasm is a bitter, irony-tinged remark. Baum writes, "When the whites win a fight, it is a victory, and when the Indians win it, it is a massacre."

Reverse psychology is the illogical or obnoxious advocacy of a specific course of action in order to persuade others to pursue the opposite. Baum writes: "Having wronged them for centuries, we had better follow it up by one more wrong, and wipe out these untamable creatures from the face of the earth."

The reference to *My Gun is Quick* and *Vengeance is Mine* is a tribute to Mickey Spillane, who must have had fun writing his books. The frontispiece to "Notes and Bibliography" is Mary Cowles Clark's depiction of the defeat of the Awgwas. Looks to me like an unretouched snapshot of Siegfried and Fafner. But not to Thos. St. John, who claims the slain Awgwas represent Native Americans. He must be kidding. You decide. Following is the complete text of the two Baum editorials which provoked the contemporary academic jihad. Read, and again decide for yourself.

From the *Aberdeen Saturday Pioneer*, Dec. 20, 1890:

Sitting Bull, most renowned Sioux of modern history, is dead. He was an Indian with a white man's spirit of hatred and revenge for those who had wronged him and his. In his day he saw his son and his tribe gradually driven from their possessions: forced to give up their old hunting grounds and espouse the hard working and uncongenial avocations of the whites. And these, his conquerors, were marked in their dealings with his people by selfishness, falsehood and treachery. What wonder that his wild nature, untamed by years of subjection, should still revolt? What wonder that a fiery rage still burned within his breast and that he should seek every opportunity of obtaining vengeance upon his natural enemies. The proud spirit of the original owners of these vast prairies inherited through centuries of fierce and bloody wars for their possession, lingered last in the bosom of Sitting Bull. With his fall the nobility of the Redskin is extinguished, and what few are left are a pack of whining curs who lick the hand that smites them. The Whites, by law of conquest, by justice of civilization, are masters *of the American continent, and the best safety of the frontier settlements will be secured by the total annihilation of the few remaining Indians. Why not annihilation? Their glory has fled, their spirit broken, their manhood effaced; better that they die than live the miserable wretches that they are. History would forget these latter despicable beings, and speak, in later ages of the glory of these grand Kings of forest and plain that Cooper loved to heroize. We cannot honestly regret their extermination, but we at least do justice to the manly characteristics possessed, according to their lights and education, by the early Redskins of America.* #

From the *Aberdeen Saturday Pioneer*, Jan. 3, 1891:

The peculiar policy of the government in employing so weak and vacillating a person as General Miles to look after the uneasy

Indians, has resulted in a terrible loss of blood to our soldiers, and a battle which, at best, is a disgrace to the war department. There has been plenty of time for prompt and decisive measures, the employment of which would have prevented this disaster. The PIONEER has before declared that our only safety depends upon the total extermination of the Indians. Having wronged them for centuries we had better, in order to protect our civilization, follow it up by one more wrong and wipe these untamed and untamable creatures from the face of the earth. In this lies safety for our settlers and the soldiers who are under incompetent commands. Otherwise, we may expect future years to be as full of trouble with the redskins as those have been in the past. An eastern contemporary, with a grain of wisdom in its wit, says that "when the whites win a fight, it is a victory, and when the Indians win it, it is a massacre." #

The only place in this book you can hear my own StraightArrow voice is probably in this Baum Philippic, where I presume to speak for a dead genius and contrarian who is not around to defend himself. Why did he ultimately choose to write for children? Obviously because he could make a comfortable living at it. But perhaps it also generated profound satisfaction to be able to stimulate young humanbeans with their minds still receptive to radical notions such as *whatsoever things are honest.*

THE BUGBY LEGACY commentary

What have we here? Just a bit of friendly josh inspired by an astoundingly successful old SciFi regular and hustler who deduced that the best business around is organized religion, and proceeded to establish his own.[3]

---

[3] I saw this mesmerizing redheaded giant on stage in Oakland, in 1951, hypnotizing volunteers from the audience and convincing them that their IQ's had advanced 40 pts. Affidavits in the foyer attested to prior achievements in this area. He was hawking his bible that pointed the way. Step right up! For

Filchings, allusions, trivia: The photo of Goshen is actually one of the Isle D'If, of Monte Cristo notoriety, and the Ancient Curse bears a remarkable resemblance to a certain secret society's loyalty oath. You guessed it: *The Mystic Knights of the Sea.*

The sheep, camels, oxen and asses referred to are Job's reward for successful completion of Yahweh's Misery Marathon.

Seeking to restore the vision of the great King Nimrod (thwarted by Yahweh the Destroyer), Ludvic Zamenhof was the father of Esperanto.

Pierre Proudhon and others did aver that property is theft, or words to that effect, but as to Charlemagne and the dog-on-three-legs gag, just kidding.

"...the Happy Few, the Band o' Winners!" sounds even *Shakespearean*, wot?

Singe méchant ("naughty monkey") is a direct burgle from Craig Ferguson. There are numerous tributes to this nimble latenight Scot scattered throughout these pages. Find them all and treat your mcpipe to a bag o' haggis.

As to the state lottery, my nephew Joaquín says it's a tax on the most gullible amongst us. Myself, I would simply class it as another pernicious and regressive "sin" tax, beloved by those who are so good at inveigling others to pick up the tab.

Of course Lincoln and GWB weren't the only kings to lie to their expendable pawns on the front lines in order to further the interests of the knights and the bishops skulking around their fortified castles. Please check out *A People's History of the United States* by Howard Zinn (Harper, 1995) and *Human Smoke* by Nicholson Baker (Simon & Schuster, 2008) for an invigorating experience in bahumbug history.

---

analysis, see Martin Gardner's *Fads and Fallacies in the Name of Science* (Dover Publications, 1957).

BACKMATTER *commentary*

(Comments on comments? Just kidding.)

ANSWERS TO RIDDLE-ME-REES POSED ON REAR ENDPAPERS

Scenario One: The initial odds are indeed one out of three for each contender. As we now know Milliwit's name was one of the two names shredded, his odds in fact are now zero. However, we also know that the order of the shredding of the two losers was random, and that by Alubat's own request, if his was the first name shredded, Laya would be obliged to name the second loser. No matter what, Laya could *not* announce Alubat's name. Therefore, the 1/3 odds that belonged to Milliwit now have passed on to Scaevola (whose name *could* have been the one announced), and he now enjoys a 2/3 advantage. Alubat's chances remain at 1/3. You agree, of course, that when all possibilities for an outcome are considered, the sum of their odds is one.

Scenario Two: This one is so hoary that I'm sure any explanation is gratuitous. Scaevola can simply ask either of them, "If I ask you if my yarmulke is white, would you say yes?" Whether truthteller or liar, if the answer is "yes," his yarmulke is white. If "no," it's black. There are other possible questions that would work.

Acknowledgments

The illustrations in this book are primarily the work of Rogelio Naranjo, world class cartoonist from Michoacán, México. He studied painting in Morelia with Alfredo Zalce, and went on to Mexico City, where he pursued an awardwinning career as a political cartoonist for major publications in that city. He is the author of several books, most recently *Me Van a Extrañar* (Editorial Proceso, 2006).

All of Naranjo's original drawings were commissioned by the author, appearing in Mexico City within a promotional pamphlet *Programación y Análisis – Campo Abierto a Nuevas Profesiones* (Datamex, 1969). The relevance of these drawings to the contents of the book in your hands is remarkable, don't you agree? I'm sure all you PhDs in Compuspeak have noticed that Naranjo's image representing the computer is of the analog tribe, rakishly retro even at the time. I couldn't possibly have invented a more stylish metaphor for this book.

I accept all responsibility, however, for the insertion of text in his drawings. To adapt them to the book I did modify five of Naranjo's original sketches as follows:

"If HE Didn't, Who Did?" Two "computer scientist" faces were altered to appear as Harry Clootie and Yam Snosnibor (in turn these were borrowed from Charles Kahles' Rudolph Rassendale, and Max Fleischer's Betty Boop, respectively).

"#@*#!!" The tutor's face was replaced with a caricature of John Foster Dulles (lifted from an issue of the *National Guardian* of the 1950's) and Al Capp's Moonbeam McSwine appears on the "Domino" jacket as the dolled-up Bergsma.

The hortatory sermon illustrated in the "Pontifications" drawing as an Escheresque speechballoon is courtesy of Saul Steinberg (*The Labyrinth,* Harper, 1960*).*

"The Bugby Legacy:" computer's tongue modified to appear as torn from its roots.

"Graduation Ceremony:" a tasseled gradcap was added to the image of *The Thinker*.

In the intro to "Mr. Vici ..." the drawing of Tik-Tok is by Jno. R. Neill, from Baum's *Ozma of Oz* (Reilly & Lee, 1907). The spaceship is from Dick Calkins' *Buck Rogers and the Doom Comet* (Whitman, 1935).

Artwork for "Perils of Satire" and "Notes & Bibliography" is by Mary Cowles Clark, appearing in L. Frank Baum's *Life and Adventures of Santa Claus (*Bowen-Merrill, 1902).

The lyrics to *God Save the Queen* appearing at the conclusion of "Mr. Vici Forms a Coalition" are often included as the second verse of the national anthem of Great Britain, although prissy Prince Charles complained that this text is "politically incorrect," and this verse is not included on the official royal government website. Thinskinned Welshmen, assuming they are being characterized as knaves, find it offensive and boo when it is sung at football (soccer) games. Authorship of the lyrics unknown, but it is interesting that the phrase "God Save the King" does appear in 1, 2 Samuel and 2 Kings (KJV).

The terms appearing in the index are identical to "The Great Ideas" listed in Robert Maynard Hutchins' *Great Books of the Western World* (Encyclopedia Britannica, Inc., 1952). A truly amazing coincidence.

And a rousing "Bless you, padre" to Bishop Baker for his rosy and entirely solicited words in the frontmatter of this book. Our modest author couldn't have said it better himself without a dollop of selfserving tarnish. On Amazon.com the Bishop ranks as 52,000[th] Reviewer of

Books, with an impressive 2,200 hits on his "Listomania" contributions. The good Bishop's biosketch reveals the following: "On reading *Cat's Cradle*, I converted to Bokononism and was inducted into the orders, rising quickly to assume the bishopric of Crocker-Amazon. I spend much of my time on the top of Mt. Davidson with Vonnegut's book as a pillow, communing with St. Francis in-the-fog. Favorite hobby: Eucharist celebration, lite on the bones and generous with the blood. Boku-maru is lots of fun, too." As a *DECLAMATORY THOUGHT FOR THE NEW MILLENNIUM* he has selected two verses from The Book of Percybysshe:

Men of Bugbog, wherefore plough for the lords who lay thee low? Wherefore weave with toil and care the rich robes your tyrants wear?

Wherefore feed, and clothe, and save, from the cradle to the grave, those ungrateful drones who would drain your sweat – nay, drink your blood?

When I joshingly commented to this seditious clergyman that he would be dubbed "The Red Dean of Haight-Ashbury," the riposte-ready prelate quipped, "Better red than dead-in-the-head."

In so many ways I am indebted to my entire family for their patience, encouragement and insights. I offer a toast to my wife Virgita, our kids, grandkids, and of course to the memory of my mom and dad, for making this trek through the valley of humbuggery a piece of cake. *A Newer Testament* is dedicated to my energetic grandsons, Ariel and Tilo, relief runners to the future. Cheers!

Biographical Note

In his hour upon the stage, Reneau H. Reneau developed a repertory that included appearances strutting as preacher's kid and then PFC, sawing the air as U.S. History teacher and computer instructor, fretting as programmer and systems analyst, and bellowing as a judgmental welfare case worker. Venues include Ft. Lewis, Maryland, Mexico, and California. In the fifties he edited and contributed to *The Torquasian Times* in Santa Cruz, and to *The Oxford Accent* in Berkeley. While in Mexico in the seventies, he wrote and published *Programación de Computadoras* and *Misanthropoesy*. Now in Los Angeles, in 2003 he authored *Misanthropology: A Florilegium of Bahumbuggery*.

Days of *Vino y Rosas*
Mexico City, 1970

Let Sound the Pomp and Circumstance No. 1!

Surprise! Here is an unannounced, unadvertised BONANZA for the purchaser of this book. It is offered in gratitude as a gift from a generous publisher to a deserving and discerning reader. Never in publishing history has a gift of this significance been presented without fanfare, without crass commercial enticement as an incentive for you to buy a book for any reason other than its own merit. By exchanging the coin representing the sweat of your brow for this assuming volume, you have revealed yourself to be a deserving recipient of this unprecedented honor.

 The honorable institution OKEFENOKEE U., an enlightened member of Academia, recognizes *LIFE EXPERIENCE* as a vital contributor to academic achievement, and your decision to consummate this purchase in itself qualifies you for a B.S. degree in Misanthropology. Go directly to DRUMROLL PARAGRAPH below.

However, to qualify for the MBA you *must* first read "The Bugby Legacy." That's all, but it's a REQUIREMENT. Then you may proceed to the DRUMROLL PARAGRAPH below.

For the impressive Ph.D. in CompuSpeak, you are obliged to submit to a departmental examination, which appears below. This examination is administered on the "honor system," and no skullduggery will be tolerated. Any rumor of deviance from strict academic probity will be reported to

Mrs. Defarge for appropriate action. Do not even attempt this examination until you have read and thoroughly parsed "Mr. Vici Forms a Coalition."

Those who aspire to the A.A. in Skinneritis, a discipline requiring considerable imagination, will expect to find that the bar is raised. The aspirant to A.A. status must resolve a knotty conundrum posed by Asar Alubat in his trailblazing textbook *See Spot Smell! See Spot Smell Jane's Fuzzy Armpit!* The A.A. conundrum follows the Doctoral Exam. You must undo the knot in an appropriate time. No Googling allowed.

DOCTORAL EXAMINATION: Note: You may skip the first question if you have difficulty grasping it and then return to it after tackling the second poser. There is no time limit.
1. What does CRAL CAVINU spell backwards?
2. How many beans make five?
On grandma's approval of your answers, you may skip to the DRUMROLL PARAGRAPH below.

(The answer to #1 is on page 102, but remember NO PEEKING IS ALLOWED. Your grandmother may check to see if your answer is correct. The answer to #2 is only hinted at in *So This Is Arcturus*, but grandma, by virtue of *LIFE EXPERIENCE*, will know the answer.

A.A. CONUNDRUM: What do you get if you cross a buzzbug with a diet colt? The answer is Buzz Liteyear, and/or a bugling. Your task is to explain the transition, i.e., derive the middle term. Grandma, don't help him on this one. An appropriate time limit of one hour (i.e. 50 minutes) is allowed. If you don't get it, consider an unrelated profession. You don't need an A.A. to be, for example, an expert witness. CANDIDATE READ NOT THE NEXT PARAGRAPH OR SUFFER THE ANCIENT CURSE OF THE INSTITUTIONALIZED MYSTIC NITS. If your grandma and your conscience attest that you have completed the requirements for a degree, you may proceed to DRUMROLL PARAGRAPH below.

[Hint to grandma. You can Google it and find the answer at Amazon.com in Bishop Baker's review of David Mamet's *Wilson* (Overlook Press, 2001). If the review has vanished in the ether by now, try this: *A diet colt is by definition a lite yearling. Crossing a buzz-bug with a liteyear-ling generates a Buzz Liteyear and/or a bugling.*]

DRUMROLL PARAGRAPH: As you complete the requisites for the corresponding diploma, you are authorized to copy and print same, with your name inscribed. It can be found on the following pages. Still eager for additional testimonial to scholastic achievement? Go back and follow the instructions to qualify for the desired degree. You will dazzle siblings, potential employers, and grandmothers for the remainder of your days, or theirs.

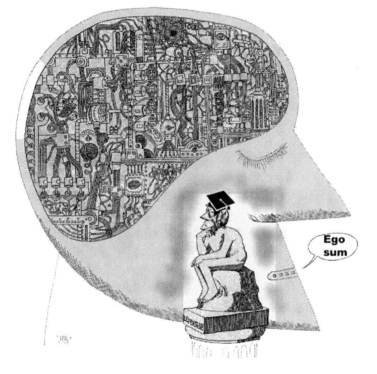

*"I have considered all discourse proclaimed
under the bugbog sun; and, behold, all is bullshit."*

THE REGENTS OF OKEFENOKEE U.

ON THE NOMINATION OF THE FACULTY OF THE

COLLEGE OF LETTERS AND SCIENCE

HAVE CONFERRED UPON

THE DEGREE OF B.S.

IN MISANTHROPOLOGY

WITH ALL THE RIGHTS AND PRIVILEGES THERETO PERTAINING

GIVEN AT OKEFENOKEE THIS SEVENTEENTH DAY OF JUNE IN THE YEAR

TWO THOUSAND AND EIGHT

Reneau H. Reneau

PROFESSOR OF BAHUMBUGGERY

Goneril O'Nuker

COMMISSIONER OF QUALITY CONTROL

Yam Snesnibor

PARALEGAL COUNSELOR

Mrs. Defarge

LOYALTY POLICE

GREAT SEAL OF OKEFENOKEE U.

echo puro pedo en lugar de cagazón

THE REGENTS OF OKEFENOKEE U.

ON THE NOMINATION OF THE FACULTY OF THE

COLLEGE OF LETTERS AND SCIENCE

HAVE CONFERRED UPON

THE DEGREE OF

MASTER OF BUSINESS ALCHEMY

WITH ALL THE RIGHTS AND PRIVILEGES THERETO PERTAINING

GIVEN AT OKEFENOKEE THIS SEVENTEENTH DAY OF JUNE IN THE YEAR

TWO THOUSAND AND EIGHT

Charles Bugby

SUCCESSFUL PRACTITIONER

Goneril O'Nuker

COMMISSIONER OF QUALITY CONTROL

Yam Snosnibor

PARALEGAL COUNSELOR

Mrs. DeForge

LOYALTY POLICE

GREAT SEAL OF OKEFENOKEE U.

echo puro pedo en lugar de cagazón

THE REGENTS OF OKEFENOKEE U.

ON THE NOMINATION OF THE FACULTY OF THE

COLLEGE OF LETTERS AND SCIENCE

HAVE CONFERRED UPON

THE DEGREE OF DOCTOR OF PHILOSOPHY

IN COMPUSPEAK

WITH ALL THE RIGHTS AND PRIVILEGES THERETO PERTAINING

GIVEN AT OKEFENOKEE THIS SEVENTEENTH DAY OF JUNE IN THE YEAR

TWO THOUSAND AND EIGHT

Billy Brutus

CHAIR, MEMORY DUMP ANALYSIS

Goneril O'Nuker

COMMISSIONER OF QUALITY CONTROL

Yam Snosnibor

PARALEGAL COUNSELOR

Mrs. Defarge

LOYALTY POLICE

GREAT SEAL OF OKEFENOKEE U.

echo para pedo en lugar de corazón

THE REGENTS OF OKEFENOKEE U.

ON THE NOMINATION OF THE FACULTY OF THE

COLLEGE OF LETTERS AND SCIENCE

HAVE CONFERRED UPON

THE DEGREE OF ASSOCIATE IN ARTS

IN SKINNERITIS

WITH ALL THE RIGHTS AND PRIVILEGES THERETO PERTAINING

GIVEN AT OKEFENOKEE THIS SEVENTEENTH DAY OF JUNE IN THE YEAR

TWO THOUSAND AND EIGHT

Asar Aluba

CHAIR, CHILD MANIPULATION STUDIES

Generil O'Nuber

COMMISSIONER OF QUALITY CONTROL

GREAT SEAL OF OKEFENOKEE U.

echa pura poba en lugar de pagado

Yam Snosnibor

PARALEGAL COUNSELOR

Mrs. Defarge

LOYALTY POLICE

Index

Two Riddle-Me-Rees for Jaded Commuters

TRY THIS SCENARIO: Princess Laya declares the yarmulke contest null! And void, as no clear winner emerges. Therefore there will be a name-drawing shootout to determine the winner of the coveted Certificate of Merit suitable for framing, although we all know it's not the prize, it's the egoboo. Each of the three contenders has written his name on a slip of paper, which is folded and placed into an upside-down yarmulke. Now the glory will depend not upon skill but on the luck of the draw or, if you prefer, on the whim of Jehovah. Princess Laya draws a slip, reads its contents, consigns the slip to her bosom, glances at and randomly relegates the other two slips, one at a time, to a nearby shredder. To allow tension and excitement to build fervor, Princess Laya decides to postpone the announcement of the result for an hour. A nervous Reddy Milliwit decides he needs to go to the toilet, and a suspicious Admiral Scaevola follows. Asar Alubat, seizing the moment, whispers to Laya, "Tell me, Princess, will I be the Anointed One?" She replies, "Don' even ask!" Unfazed, he rejoins, "Well then don't tell me my name, but at least tell me the name on the first slip you so randomly shredded <u>that wasn't me</u>." Laya thinks fast. "Well O.K, you sillyBilly, that would be ... Reddy Milliwit!" Inwardly, Alubat is a furnace of exultation. With that, Laya retires to the ladies' lair, and when Scaevola emerges from the men's den, Alubat cannot contain himself. "My glorious Admiral! You and I are still in the running! The Princess has confided to me that Milliwit will get no certificate to hang on his grandma's fridge, and thus the probability of a favorable outcome for either your worship or me has augmented from a paltry one-out-of-three to a contentious one-out-of-two! Congrats, *mi jefe*, and may